CONCILIUM

CONCILIUM 2009/3

ECO-THEOLOGY

Edited by
Elaine Wainwright, Luiz Carlos Susin,
and Felix Wilfred

SCM Press · London

Published by SCM Press, 13–17 Long Lane, London EC1A 9PN

Copyright © International Association of Conciliar Theology, Madras (India)

www.concilium.in

English translations copyright © 2009 SCM-Canterbury Press Ltd

ISBN 978 0 334 03104 8

Printed in the UK by
CPI Antony Rowe, Chippenham SN14 6LH

Concilium published March, June, August, October,
December

Contents

Editorial

The new millennium opened with hope and expectations. A new dawning, a new future was dreamed and imagined. Within a few short years, however, the planet has experienced some of the most devastating groanings in recorded human history. The Tsunami of 2004 shocked the world. This was followed by a huge earthquake in Northern Pakistan; Hurricane Katrina inundated New Orleans, displacing almost an entire city; Cyclone Nargis devastated the Irrawaddy Delta of Burma/Myanmar, leaving thousands of people dead; and only days later the Province of Sichuan in China was rocked by an earthquake in which thousands died, especially children. Most recently southern and northern states of Australia have been devastated by some of the worst fires and floods in human memory.

This volume of *Concilium* has been developed in response to the increasing urgency of these groanings of Earth. It is carrying forward, with a different focus, the discussions initiated in an earlier issue of *Concilium* in 1995, edited by Leonardo Boff and Virgil Elizondo. Recently experienced ecological devastation is calling for new theological responses both in the academy and at the grass roots, as witnessed by the most recent gathering of the World Forum on Theology and Liberation in Belém do Pará, Brazil, from 21 to 25 January 2009. The foci of its major panels were 'Spirituality and Ethics in the Sustainability Agenda' and the 'Eco-theological Dimension of Embodiment' – themes that also informed many workshops. These ecological concerns dovetailed with those of the World Social Forum, which drew thousands to Belém around climate and environmental issues, with a particular reference to the Amazonian region in which both fora were held.

This volume seeks to provide readers with insights for a theological response to ecological issues that have developed since 1995. It opens with Elaine Wainwright's question – how shall we read the book of the genealogy, which introduces Matthew's Gospel, in an age of ecological crisis? This article recognizes the urgency and the interconnectedness of current ecological crises at a time when the global economy is under serious threat. The ethical and moral issues being raised by many invite theologians to enter into the conversation. Wainwright contends that a new way of thinking – namely, ecological thinking – needs to guide readings of Christianity's sacred story, and she shows how to read with environmental sensitivity the gospel narrative, even where a passage seems to be so explicitly human-centered as in the case of genealogy.

Leonardo Boff surveys the challenges to ecological thinking and the development of eco-theology. The author, who has been pursuing eco-theology since the 1980s, takes up the theory of *Gaia* to underline the fundamental relationship of humanity to the Earth. According to the new paradigm we are all children and members of the Earth; and she is our mother, and we all belong to the same family. In support of this paradigm we have many solid scientific facts, which should have its impact on the ethics of human relationship to all creatures.

Some of the complexity of the theological response to ecological crises and the questions they raise emerge in the next three articles in the volume. Anne Elvey is confronted by the devastating fires that ravaged her home state of Victoria in southern Australia in February 2009. She recognizes the ways such experiences may turn those of the human community who have believed themselves to have mastery of their contexts to look anew to the experience of the biblical writers who were more attentive to Earth's elements and the human community in such material contexts. The question that confronts us is how we can or ought to name God in the face of the questions which Earth's groaning place before us at present. In exploring this she moves toward proposing a new attitude of a humility before the very materiality that is all around us. This may provide a pathway along which, at some future time, it may be possible to speak of God ecologically. At present, we may need to remain silent.

Felix Wilfred advocates the need for an inter-religious eco-theology that would be in dialogue with other religious traditions and draw inspiration from their resources. In this context he calls for a critical re-examination of the Christian tradition, especially in regard to the understanding of salvation. Other religious traditions are crucial today for the salvation of the Earth, without which there will be no human salvation. The holistic vision and a harmonious approach to nature that Hinduism, Buddhism, Daoism, etc. offer should help us overcome an exploitative anthropocentrism and inflated historical consciousness.

Epistemological questions arise for the theologians who are beginning to think ecologically, and Alirio Cáceres Aguirre addresses these. After reviewing some of the unfortunate ecological discourses that are at the same time ambiguous, the author opens up the different possible theological discourse with reference to a few authors on the subject. His conclusion is very clear: there is an urgent need to change the analytical and instrumental *logos* by the *symbolic logos*.

Eco-theology cannot be restricted to theological communities of scholars but must find expression in the praxis of the *ekklesia*. It is only communities engaging in new ways with all their constituent members that will go beyond the human community to create together a different future for the Earth and for the human family. And so praxis is a necessary element in responding to Earth's groaning. Jacques Haers addresses such praxis in general terms, setting out first four important lessons learned from Europe's recent history of violence, domination, and colonialism. These lessons lead him to propose new ways of responding to the acute ecological challenges, responding as Churches, as communities of faith by way of processes that he calls *ecclesio-genesis*.

While Haers proposes very broad sweeping responses from religious communities, especially those shaped by the theology of the Christian *ekklesia*, Neil Darragh's proposals are much more specific: giving attention to the public dimension of spirituality and evoking traditions of asceticism, which, like Elvey's suggestion that we reactivate humility, reclaims central values and practices of Christianity but now in a new key informed by an ecological consciousness.

The emergence of eco-feminist consciousness and praxis by way of summer schools and workshops involving exploration of myth, participation in ritual and embodied engagement demonstrate very explicitly some of the general claims made in previous papers. Mary Judith Ress details some of the pathways toward ecological conversion taken by Latin American women from two women's collectives, *Con-spirando* and *Capacitar-Chile*. The new anthropology, cosmology, and epistemology emerging from the work of the summer schools are explored by Ress in the second segment of her article through the words of women participants themselves whom she interviewed. One might ask whether the discernment and the *ecclesiogenesis* proposed by Haers are indeed visible here in microcosm.

John Clammer also recognizes the need for praxis, in particular through education. He draws our attention to the ambiguous role played by religion both as legitimizing exploitation of the Earth as well as having been sources of ethics. The challenge today is that of praxis, which leads him to pose the critical question whether theological education and education in general today are attuned to construct the different paradigm of relationship we require vis-à-vis the Earth. We face a pedagogical challenge. He advocates the need for 'a new eco-centered approach to education in general, a new role for theology as the most potentially integrative of all the disciplines, and an overcoming of the ancient dichotomies of sacred/secular, material/spiritual'.

The second part of the issue, Theological Forum, narrates, discusses, and reflects some experiences and practices. Many individuals and groups are responding to the Church's call to an ecological conversion in a variety of ways. Josias da Costa Júnior responds to the challenge by proposing a theology of creation for today. The author explores two possible methods in relating the scientific data with the biblical tradition. According to him, Leonardo Boff underlines the knowledge and data through science as reflective of the transcendence in immanence of the universe. Moltmann on his part follows a methodology of dialogue with the Jewish religious thought of creation to be able to contribute to science.

Sr Dorothy Stang was an activist for the sake of the planet, especially the Amazon River. For many years, she stood as a fearless defender of the poor peasants in the state of Pará, Amazon region, Brazil. Her involvement for their cause brought her in confrontation with loggers who denuded the forests and the landowners who exploited the poor. This led to her assassination on 12 February 2005. Luiz Carlos Susin reflects on the significance of this ecological martyrdom.

The question of education raised by Clammer finds an encouraging response in the contribution of Marian O'Sullivan, who reflects on the educational role played by the experiment at *An Tairseach* farm in Ireland. This ecological experiment, spearheaded by Irish Dominican Sisters, consists of organic farming, wild-life conservation, and creation of a Centre for Ecology and Spirituality. This experiment is a sign of hope, especially for creating a new pedagogy and ecological consciousness. It draws from the Christian tradition of wisdom regarding Earth and nature. Then an Indian scientist, Jayapaul Azariah, shows that, from the knowledge available, Earth is the only planet that supports life-forms; he stresses the importance of ethically and rationally managing the available resources of water, food, etc., which nature provides only in a restricted measure.

The issue concludes with a contribution from Jill Gowdie, who recalls the moving experience of the World Youth Day held in Sydney in 2008 with the presence of the Pope. She narrates what the pilgrimage to World Youth Day meant for the participants of her group. Reflecting on the significance of the event, she notes that one could experience the presence of Jesus in the sea of young people that filled the city of Sydney, in the mystical communion and community one could experience, and the transformative action the event called for.

We hope that the reflections presented here will generate a lot of discussion in theological circles and bring about fresh theological perspectives. It is also hoped that the contributions in this number will serve as a source of encouragement and support to and among all those are deeply involved in nurturing the Earth.

We should like to thank the following for their help and suggestions: Diego Irrarazábal, Mary E. Hunt, Marcio Fabri, Paul Burns.

Elaine Wainwright, Luiz Carlos Susin, Felix Wilfred

1. Earth Challenges Theology: Listening to the Voices

The Book of the Genealogy: How Shall We Read It?

ELAINE WAINWRIGHT

I. Crisis: crucial turning point or sign of impending disaster

If we were to consider our time, the now of 2009 in the unfolding or expanding¹ of planet Earth, as a moment in 'the book of the genealogy' of Earth, how would we read it, with whom would we read it, on whose account would we read it? Would this moment, this *krisis*, be a sign of impending disaster or a crucial turning point? These are but some of the urgent questions that the current global ecological and economic crises raise for the theologian, for the biblical scholar concerned with the book, with the text, with the sacred story of Christianity.

In February 2009 the southern Australian state of Victoria suffered the worst bushfires on record, with the loss of 210 human and countless animal lives, over 2000 homes and myriads of habitats destroyed, more than 450,000 hectares of land devastated, and 7,000 people and untold wildlife left homeless. At the same time, much of north Queensland was struck by floods that devastated the land and, while the loss of human life was lower than in the Victorian fires, caused the death of numerous animals and other members of the area's fragile ecosystems, as indeed did the fires. Analysts asked whether these extremes of flood and fire, which in themselves are part of Australia's natural ecological systems, were the result of climate change.

Such disasters highlight the challenges to governments internationally in the face of a wide range of such occurrences, and the Australian government is no stranger to such challenges. It has set a target to cut greenhouse gas emissions by 5 per cent by 2020 (or by 15 per cent only if there is more wide-spread international commitment to tougher measures). Not only is their target critiqued by the Australian Green Party, whose goal is 25 per cent, but the environmental group *Get Up Action for Australia* has launched a campaign to challenge the Australian Government in relation to their low target and the way this is being lowered even further by their permitting businesses to trade permits in ways that offset the savings made by individual citizens.[2]

In the broader region of Oceania, climate change and resultant rises in sea levels are creating new waves of migration – that of climate refugees. One of the most threatened groups at present, indeed they are being named as the first climate refugees,[3] are the 1,400 residents of the Cartaret Islands, 86 kilometres north east of Bougainville, whom the Autonomous Bougainville Government is currently seeking to settle on Bougainville because of the rising sea levels submerging their atolls.[4] The rising sea levels threaten not only human communities but also the ecosystems of these island and atolls, and the resultant loss of habitat for many species supported within these systems is having effects long-term we cannot now know. What we do know, however, is that the climate refugees are not only human populations but also birds and other animals whose habitats have been destroyed and who now wander in search of a new home.

Aspects of climate change are among the many daily challenges to the very survival, not to mention the flourishing, of planet Earth. These changes are intimately linked to a wide range of other issues, but the human community has in recent times been faced with a new challenge, a global economic crisis. One wonders and even perhaps fears that ecological issues, which were beginning to be given attention not only by world leaders but also by a wide range of organizations as well as individuals in their daily lives, will be set aside in the face of this global economic crisis facing most countries as they enter 2009.[5] Or does the current situation provide an invitation to change?

As recently as January 2009 Michael Smith wrote that '[a] huge rethink is going on about the values that underpin the whole capitalist system in the light of the global economic crisis.'[6] He cites Oxford Professor Timothy Garton-Ash who, writing in the *Guardian* on 1 January 2009, raises these questions: 'How much more in money and things do we need? Is enough as good as a feast? Could we manage with less? What really matters to you? What contributes most to your individual happiness?' Such reflections and questions demonstrate that theology, concerned as it is with moral issues and ethical values, has a place, even an urgent place, with and among other disciplines in facing the current global crisis.

In this article, I seek to reflect on the challenges that the current interlocking of global movements discussed briefly above is posing for biblical scholars. An examination of possible responses in this field of study will indicate how such scholars can participate with other theologians and researchers from a range of disciplines in the current moral and ethical discourse that is necessary for the survival of Earth. I evoke the phrase 'book of the genealogy', which opens the Gospel of Matthew (1:1) and which echoes Genesis 2.4 and 5.1–2, and I ask shall we or how shall we read such texts in the current global context and its challenge to ethical and moral values.

II. Toward ecological reading

Biblical studies are concerned with a story, a sacred story that is ancient, arising out of cultures and cosmologies that differ profoundly from those of the contemporary Earth story provided by cosmologists and evolutionary biologists. And yet this sacred story has always been interpreted and reinterpreted, told and retold in the face of ever new contexts. Most recently, biblical scholars have participated in such re-tellings in the contexts of the liberation movements of the second half of the twentieth century, the feminist movement of that same period, and a little later post-colonialism and the growing awareness of indigenous cultures and their interpretive frameworks. The question raised by the ecological crisis is whether ecology can simply be added to the various approaches of contextual theology or to the justice paradigm that informs them or whether something new is called for. In order to address this question, I will lay out briefly two analyses of current approaches within eco-theology.

The eco-feminist theologian Heather Eaton and eco-theologian John Haught have both recognized a tradition-based or apologetic approach to the cry of Earth.[7] In biblical studies such an approach has resulted in a focus on texts such as Genesis 1 or Psalm 8, which are read as providing a positive affirmation of Earth. Simply focusing on such positive elements in the biblical story or Christian tradition, however, does not take account of the insufficiencies within it in the face of the new ecological questions, especially the anthropocentrism woven into narratives and texts whose focus is predominantly the human-human and human-divine nexus. This has resulted in a text and a history of interpretation characterized by widespread ignoring or negating of Earth apart from its human constituents. The *earth-centred* approach identified by Eaton, which Haught calls a *sacramental* approach, takes account of the extraordinary Earth story that has come to us in recent decades from cosmologists and evolutionary biologists and the ways this invites new explorations of the tradition. For some biblical scholars, this has meant a critical approach to the entire biblical text that seeks not only to read against the grain of the text when it negates any aspects of Earth but also to read with and for Earth in clearly Earth-identified texts but also in the biblical story as a whole.[8]

One of the questions that such a shift in theological perspective raises, especially among those who have been engaged in such a critical approach to reading the biblical text through the liberation, feminist, post-colonial, and indigenous movements, is whether the ecological approach is another prong so-to-speak in the justice paradigm or whether there is a more significant shift being called for. The focus within these movements for justice has generally been justice within the human community and this remains significant in seeking ecological justice. The ecological crisis and the new Earth story, however, challenge us to a new perspective that recognizes the anthropocentrism woven into not only most Western cultures but most of the world's cultures today. In order to undertake ecological readings of the biblical text or the Christian tradition, a new way of thinking is necessary. Such a shift in thinking can then inform the justice paradigm and can incorporate the very important justice perspectives in the feminist, post-colonial, and other liberationist approaches. This, however, is different from an approach that would simply add ecology as an issue to current critical frameworks. It is only by shifting human consciousness or human thinking that informs biblical reading that a truly ecological reading can be undertaken.

Lorraine Code has explored just such a shift, proposing *ecological thinking* as a new social imaginary that seeks to move beyond the social imaginary of mastery that has dominated for so long and which underpins the metaphors, images, ways of thinking and practices that have caused and continue to cause ecological damage and destruction.[9] Indeed, she is suggesting that the human community is yearning and groaning toward this new imaginary that will be characterized by the complexity and the delicate interrelatedness that constitutes ecosystems. It will be concerned with the ways in which place or habitat for all Earth constituents requires attention not only to location but also to the temporal, social, and cultural interactions enacted there – the way in which nature and the environment are woven into culture and all its complexities. The human community cannot be separated from its relationships with all other Earth beings. And within such a web of relationships, critical attention needs to be given to any forms of domination or exploitation. Ecological thinking does indeed require a significant shift in consciousness, but such a shift will not negate work for justice but rather extend that work to include justice for all Earth constituents. Grounded in such a perspective or such thinking, the biblical scholar can now read ecologically as an active and multidimensional process.

Such reading will attend to the materiality of the text and materiality in the text, to place and to habitat as the complex web into which action and movement in the biblical narrative is woven. It will consider hospitality as an ecological reading category learned from Earth and it will read against the grain of those aspects of the text that elide, negate, or claim power over any of Earth's constituents. Such a reading informed by ecological thinking will enable a re-telling of Christianity's sacred story and contribute with other theological insights and reflections to addressing the urgent ethical and moral issues currently facing the Earth community.

III. The book of the genealogy – reading ecologically

The Gospel of Matthew begins with the phrase *biblos geneseōs*, the book of the genealogy (RSV). It points forward to genealogy, a specific genealogy of Jesus Christos but it also points back. It evokes the same phrase as appears in Genesis texts: the generations of the heavens and the earth (2.4) and of the human community, male and female (5.1–2). The very specificity of this book with its focus on Jesus Christos has a place not only in a particular story of human ancestry but within the story of all human ancestors as well as in the Earth story itself evoked by the 'heavens and the earth'. Genealogy can move between the particular and the universal, the human and the more-than-human others whose story, whose genealogy, goes back billions of years prior to that of the human, male and female. It is all this that the opening phrase of Matthew's Gospel evokes.

Primack and Abrams invite their readers to imagine themselves as a 'branching history' and to send their consciousness back through time at 'lightening speed' to the Big Bang.[10] They do not use the word genealogy, but such a 'branching history' or story is genealogy, that of the heavens and earth. This genealogy, like the human genealogy of Jesus, is not a utopia. Lorraine Code reminds her readers that ecosystems are 'as cruel as they are kind, as unpredictable and overwhelming as they are orderly and nurturant, as unsentimentally destructive of their less viable members as they are cooperative and mutually sustaining.'[11] Kenrick Smithyman, a New Zealand poet, captures this in poetry as he remembers some cataclysmic event in the long distant past beyond human history, which left giant kauri trees of the New Zealand forest cut down so that only traces of stump and root remain.

> Whatever happened, it happened.
> In swamp, on lowlands, gum diggers find ancestors
> Sometimes a lot of them lying the one way
> As though sometime was
> A great wind which put down a bush if not a forest.[12]

Genealogy as it is evoked at the head of the book, of the text, of the narrative of the Gospel of Matthew, draws the reader's imagination into the entire Earth story with all that is life-giving and death-dealing in its unfolding. It invites attentiveness to the life/death cycle that constitutes such unfolding and to that which is death-dealing and violent in a way that is destructive of that unfolding – the possibility that the extremes of flood and fire presently being experienced not only in Australia but around the planet are the result of unethical human behaviour that depletes Earth's resources and disturbs ecosystems.

Biblos, like *genesis* or genealogy, functions multivalently in an ecological reading of Matthew's Gospel. Prior to its designation of book or narrative, it named the bark, the inner bark of the papyrus plant from which the sheets of papyrus were made to be used as the carrier of writing, of narrative, of story (the original gospel texts would have been written on papyrus when first committed to writing). This designation carries the reader back to the papyrus plant, but also forward to the vellum of the early codices that succeeded the papyri as *biblos* and forward to the paper that carries the narrative in myriads of bibles today. In each instance, flora and fauna have given up a life to constitute this *biblos*. Such a gift invites respect and attentiveness to gift and gift-giving as well as to the possibility of exploitation of the gift as the human community devours old-growth forests to serve its needs or wants. This notion of gift and reciprocity will be key themes of the Matthean gospel narrative that follows this opening evocation and one that will require very careful and ethical attention in ecological thinking and reading today.

For the contemporary ecological reader, there is a recognition, as already indicated above in my citing of Smithman, that the biblical text not only evokes texts prior to its compilation but also those available to its current readers from a variety of fields including poetry, agrarian writing, nature writing, the arts and philosophy, and critical thinking – to name just some. Genealogy or *whakapapa* for the Maori people of New Zealand is more than family tree, as this line in Apirana Taylor's poem 'Whakapapa' indicates:

Whakapapa whakapapa ties you to the land . . .
this is your inheritance
the sky and earth and all that lies between.[13]

Family and land are intimately connected. Indeed the *tangata whenua* are
the people of the land, those whose *whakapapa* or genealogy connects them
to the land in general and a particular part of that land.

Reading the Matthean genealogy ecologically can, therefore, evoke and
invoke not just each generation as kin but also their habitat. Taking v. 2 as
an example – Abraham was the father of Isaac, and Isaac the father of Jacob,
and Jacob the father of Judah and his brothers – we recognize very readily
the socio-cultural matrix of family and the text of Genesis 12 – 50 that is
drawn into the Matthean text intertextually. But Matthew 1:2 also evokes
inter/con-textually the land of Canaan through which Abraham journeys
and in which other peoples dwell, a land that is characterized by a number
of different eco-zones.[14] At the head of the Abraham story stands the divine
demand that he leave his country or his land and go to another land that will
be shown to him. Just as it is not possible to trace the intricacies of kinship
through Genesis 12 – 50 (they are merely evoked by the short verse of Matt.
1.2) so too is it impossible to trace through all the ways in which family and
land are interconnected in those same stories. Some brief critical comments
are, however, in order.

Norman Habel draws attention to the intimate connection between the
immigrant Abrahamic family and the land. They are not threatened by evic-
tion nor do they dominate the land. Indeed, Habel claims that '[t]he ancient
trails of the ancestors and the sacred sites they establish turn the territory
into a storied landscape in which the history of Israel's beginnings is tan-
gibly recorded.'[15] What is silenced by such a story, however, is that of the
inhabitants of the land and the way that they have storied it – a way that like-
wise belongs to the genealogy of the heavens and the earth, the unfolding of
Earth's story. What is also silenced is the voice of Earth's multiple constituents telling that story. Only land is storied and that in the voice/s of a small
group of human constituents who are designated chosen.

Gene McAfee, who brings a specific ecological perspective to the reading of the origins of Israel, recognizes some of the problematics in the
Abrahamic narrative that is drawn into the Matthean Gospel inter/con-
textually. Indeed, he would see that narrative at odds with eco-justice principles, saying that '[n]one of that narrative's central concerns are focused
on the natural environment as an active participant in Abraham's story.'[16]

Examining the link between land and the fertility of a chosen group, McAfee draws the radical conclusion that '[t]he desideratum of the chosen people in a chosen land emphasizes separation, distinctiveness, hierarchical relationships and exclusiveness – a worldview that is deeply at odds with a sensibility that views interconnectedness as the fundamental fact of ecological existence.'[17] Matthean inter/con-textuality brings a warning as well as a potential to read against the grain of the Abrahamic narrative and to make a space for the silenced story of the land of Canaan and its constituents of the Abrahamic period to find their voice in our reading and the space which it creates for them.

In the contemporary context of reading ecologically, 'genealogy' or 'the book of the genealogy' may evoke another present text, in this instance Michel Foucault. Following Nietzsche, he claimed genealogy not as a 'branched history' but rather as a 'search for descent', which, in his words, 'is not the erecting of foundations: on the contrary, it disturbs what was previously considered immobile; it fragments what was thought unified; it shows the heterogeneity of what was imagined consistent in itself.'[18] Genealogy points as much to discontinuity as to continuity, as already noted above. Further, within the Matthean genealogy, the naming of five women disturbs what was considered the ideal of patriarchal descent and alerts readers to the rendering invisible of the pregnant female body of each mother and the materiality of their birth processes. Discontinuity is also present in the closing entry of the genealogy. The reader had been led to expect 'Joseph fathered Jesus', but this is not what is heard. Rather Joseph is identified in terms of his relationship to Mary of whom Jesus was born. Something different is possible in and through this birth just as something new and different is possible in and through an ecological reading of this ancient text. It is possible to rupture the social imaginary of mastery. It is possible to intervene in the effects of climate change. It is possible for one to be born of the line of Abraham and David who breaks the line of favoured reproduction in a way that gives readers pause to examine the intimate link between social reproduction giving rise to human genealogy (especially that of favoured lines) and the genealogy of the heavens and the earth, the Earth story.

The book of the genealogy in Matthew 1.1 is of Jesus Christos. Jesus who is singled out with the title *christos* or anointed one is located in an extraordinary story that stretches back over fourteen billion years and that stretches into an unknown future full of promise.[19] And Earth welcomes Jesus as a particular manifestation of God with us, God with Earth in all its unfolding (Matt. 1.23). The genealogy of the heavens and the earth embraces this

Jesus, and he is welcomed with the hospitality that the Earth community has extended and continues to extend to all its constituents. In Jesus, the God whom Haught says is 'revealed gradually in the evolution of matter, life, human culture and the religions of the world,' is manifest in a new way but not one that will be separate from matter, life, human culture and religion, but will continue grounded in the inter-relatedness of the Earth community. This story of Jesus, like that of the cosmos, will be promise of a new, a different future for the heavens and the earth and for the *anthropos*, male and female.

Conclusion: How shall we read it?

We shall read anew the book of the genealogy so that we can read it with the critical questions of a planet threatened by climate change, by human degradation of land and other natural resources, and by a range of issues resulting from a social imaginary founded on mastery, the mastery of the *anthropos* and often more particularly the mastery of the male. We shall read it anew informed by ecological thinking, a way of imagining, structuring, and living life that is contrary to the cult of mastery. We shall read it anew in dialogue with creative thinkers and writers of our time who themselves are conscious of power and mastery but also of the power and potential of stories, of cosmologies that are ancient and new. We shall read it attentive to habitat and hospitality as these are woven into an ancient text but are obscured by our anthropocentrism. We shall read it with other eco- and eco-feminist theologians, with philosophers, with the thinkers of our time who are seeking to address the ethical and moral implications of an economic and ecological crisis such that seems to leave only the hope that Earth is itself a promise of a new tomorrow.

Notes

1. I wish here to evoke the notion of an 'expanding universe' common among current cosmological scientists. See Joel R. Primack and Nancy Ellen Abrams, *The View from the Center of the Universe: Discovering Our Extraordinary Place in the Cosmos*, New York: Riverhead Books, 2006.
2. See Simon Sheikh, 'Fact Sheet on Australia's "Low" Pollution Future'. Accessed online, http://www.getup.org.au/files/campaigns/cprsfactsheet. pdf, 26 Feb. 2009.
3. Teresita Pérez, 'Climate Refugees: The Human Toll of Global Warming,' 7 Dec. 2006. Accessed online, http://www.americanprogress.org/issues/2006/12/

climate_refugees.html, 7 Mar. 2009.

4. See report of Campbell Cooney, Friday 13 Feb. 2009, 'Bougainville works to relocate "climate refugees"'. Accessed online, http://www.abc.net.au/news/stories/2009/02/13/2491415.htm, 7 Mar. 2009.

5. For a study that demonstrates that such a convergence of global issues is not new and that the current economic crisis is not just a product of this year but has been much longer in the making, see Leonardo Boff, *Global Civilization: Challenges to Society and Christianity*, trans. Alexandre Guiherme, Cross Cultural Theologies, London: Equinox, 2003.

6. Michael Smith, 'Economic crisis calls for conscience-based ecology economies.' Accessed online, http://www.forceforgood.com/Blogs/Economic-crisis-calls-for-conscience-based-ecology-economies-261/1.aspx, 7 Mar. 2009.

7. See Heather Eaton, *Introducing Ecofeminist Theologies*, Introductions in Feminist Theology 12, London: T. & T. Clark International, 2005, pp. 72–74, who calls such an approach 'tradition-centred' and John F. Haught, 'Christianity and Ecology,' in Roger S. Gottlieb (ed.) *This Sacred Earth: Religion, Nature, Environment*, New York: Routledge, 2004, pp. 235–6, who uses the term 'apologetic'.

8. See the 5-volume *Earth Bible*, ed. Norman Habel and other collaborators from the Earth Bible Team, published by Sheffield Academic Press and Pilgrim Press.

9. Lorraine Code, *Ecological Thinking: The Politics of Epistemic Location*, Studies in Feminist Theology, Oxford: Oxford University Press, 2006.

10. Primack and Abrams, *A View from the Center of the Universe*, p. 85. Such an understanding is, however, not new but characterizes many indigenous cosmologies. In New Zealand Maori traditions, '[t]he term "*Te Here Tangata*", literally "The Rope of Mankind", is also used to describe genealogy. I visualise myself with my hand on this rope which stretches into the past for the fifty or so generations that I can see, back from there to the instant of Creation, and on into the future for at least as long.' From *Whakapapa Maori: Structure, Terminology, Usage*, accessed online, http://maaori.com/whakapapa/whakpap2.htm#Introduction, 9 Mar. 2009.

11. Code, *Ecological Thinking*, p. 6.

12. Kendrick Smithyman, 'Lone Kauri', in *Atua Wera*, Auckland: Auckland University Press, 1997, p. 197.

13. Apirana Taylor, 'Whakapapa', in *Soft Leaf Falls of the Moon*, ed. Apirana Taylor, Wellington: The Pohutukawa Press, 1996, pp. 10–11.

14. David Hillel, *The Natural History of the Bible: an Environmental Exploration of the Hebrew Scriptures*, New York: Columbia University Press, 2006.

15. Norman C. Habel, *The Land is Mine: Six Biblical Land Ideologies*, Overtures to Biblical Theology. Minneapolis: Fortress, 1995, p. 119. It should be noted here that this work preceded his turn to an ecological hermeneutic.

16. Gene McAfee, 'Chosen People in a Chosen Land: Theology and Ecology in the Story of Israel's Origins', in *The Earth Story in Genesis*, ed. Norman C. Habel and Shirley Wurst, The Earth Bible 1, Sheffield: Sheffield Academic Press, 2000, p. 159.
17. McAfee, 'Chosen People', p. 174.
18. Michel Foucault, *Language, Counter-memory, Practice: selected essays and interviews*, trans. Donald F. Bouchard and Sherry Simon, Oxford: Blackwell, 1977, p. 147.
19. Haught, 'Christianity and Ecology, pp. 240–5, recognizes a third type of eco-theology grounded in the biblical narrative, namely apocalyptic. For him, this is grounded in the biblical notion of eschatology or future fulfilment and linked to his sense that the cosmos itself 'is in its deepest essence a promise of future fulfilment' (p. 240). 'What makes nature deserve our care,' he says, 'is not that it is divine but that it is pregnant with a mysterious future' (p. 245).

Earth as Gaia: An Ethical and Spiritual Challenge

LEONARDO BOFF

Until the advent of modern science with the founding fathers of the scientific paradigm, Descartes, Galileo, and above all Francis Bacon, Earth was seen as a living, shining entity, which inspired fear, respect, and veneration. Once modern instrumental-analytical reasoning had taken hold, it came to be seen simply as *res extensa*, an inert object lacking understanding, handed over to human beings so they could use it to express their will to power and for their creative and destructive intervention. This view enabled them to embrace the proposition that all its resources and services could be exploited without limitation, leading to the point we have reached – real devastation of biodiversity, upsetting the balance of eco-systems, and the rise of global warming.

As a counter-current to this destructive process, we are now, surprisingly, witnessing the emergence of a new perception that Earth and humankind share the same origin and the same fate, and that we possess the means to transform this possible tragedy into a passing crisis out of which a new paradigm of care and support for all of life may emerge. This new state of consciousness is based in the understanding developed by the earth sciences: the new biology, modern cosmology and astrophysics, and, last but by no means least, deep ecology. These have produced a new enchantment with Earth, a new utopia that can fill us with hope and encourage us to beneficial practices of recovery, conservation, and expansion of life and the Earth as a living system.

I. Earth seen from beyond Earth

The astronauts provided us with a convincing introduction to this new view, since they were able to see Earth from beyond Earth. The testimony given by Russell Scheickhart sums up many other accounts: 'Seen from the outside, you realize that everything meaningful to you – the whole of history, art, birth, death, love, joy and tears – all this is in that little blue and white point that you can cover with your thumb. And from that viewpoint you realize that everything has changed, that something new is coming into being, that the relationship is not the same as it was before.'[1]

From there, from a spaceship or from the Moon, Earth effectively emerges as one celestial body in the vast cosmic chain. It is the third planet from the sun, from a sun that is one medium-sized star among billions of other suns in our galaxy, a galaxy that is one among another hundred billion galaxies or conglomerates of galaxies. The solar system is 28,000 light years from the centre of our galaxy, the Milky Way, in the inner curve of the spiral arm of Orion.

In 1982, invited by the *New York Times* to celebrate the twenty-fifth anniversary of the launching of the first Sputnik, which inaugurated the space age, Isaac Asimov wrote that the legacy of this space quarter-century was the perception that, as seen from spaceships, Earth and humanity make up *a single entity*.[2] In other words, we form one complex, diverse, contradictory, single being, one gifted with great dynamism, which we have now become accustomed to calling Gaia.

Such an assertion means that human beings are in no sense above Earth. They are not wandering pilgrims, passers-by coming from elsewhere and belonging to other worlds. No: as *homo* (human), they come from *humus* (fertile soil); they are *Adam* (which in Hebrew means 'child of Earth'), born from *Adamah* (life-giving Earth); they are sons and daughters of Earth. Even more, they are Earth itself, which at an advanced stage of its evolution began to feel, to think, to love, and to worship. Never again can human consciousness lose sight of the fact that we are Earth and that our destiny is indissolubly linked to that of the Earth and of the cosmos of which Earth forms a part.[3]

This perception of Earth-humankind mutual belonging and organic unity derives with crystal clarity from modern genetic and molecular biology, from complexity and chaos theory.[4] The story of life is that of the emergence of a whole evolutionary process, from the most elemental energies and particles resulting from the 'big bang', through primordial gas, to supernovas, galaxies, stars, the geosphere, the hydrosphere, the atmosphere, and finally to the biosphere from which springs the anthroposphere (and, for Christians, the Christosphere) and, with globalization, the noosphere, in Teilhard de Chardin's sense.

Life, which is now 3.8 billion years old, is the complexity, self-organization, pan-relationality, and self-transcendence, the outcome of the potentialities of the universe itself. Ilya Prigogine, the Russian-Belgian chemist/physicist who was awarded the 1977 Nobel Prize for chemistry, studied how thermodynamics functions in living systems, which always present as 'open systems', which means that their equilibrium is fragile and they are permanently seeking to adapt.[5] They are continually exchanging energy with the environment. They produce entropy and at the same time escape from entropy by the process of metabolizing disorder and chaos and changing them into complex orders that self-organize, thereby avoiding entropy (producing negentropy, which is syntropy). They are endowed, Prigogine claims, with 'dissipative structures', a concept that applies to all life-processes.

For example, the sun's photons are useless to it (the sun), being energy that escapes when the hydrogen on which it lives is burned. These photons, which are disorder (detritus), serve as food for plants through the process of photosynthesis. Through this, they break down carbon dioxide, on which they feed, and liberate oxygen, which is necessary for life. So what is disorder for one entity serves as order for another. It is through a dynamic balance between order and disorder that life is maintained.[6] Disorder drives the creation of new forms of order, higher and more complex ones, which dissipate less energy. On the basis of this logic, the universe is continually progressing to ever more complex forms of life and so to a reduction of entropy.

On the human and spiritual level, forms of relationship and life originate in which syntropy predominates over entropy. Thought, solidarity, and love are very powerful energies with a low level of entropy and a high level of syntropy. From this viewpoint, we are faced not with terminal death but with the transfiguration of the cosmogenic process into supremely ordered and vital new forms of life.

II. Gaia: the new view of Earth

Life is not just *on* Earth and occupying parts of Earth (the biosphere). Earth itself, as a whole, proclaims itself to be a living macro-organism. What the mythologies of the early inhabitants of both East and West testified about Earth as Great Mother is being confirmed more and more by contemporary experimental science.[7] Witness to this are the researches of the English doctor and biologist James Lovelock, of the biologist Lynn Margulis, and others.[8] These hold the Earth to be an immense living super-organism, self-organizing and self-regulating. Lovelock propounded the Gaia hypothesis (*Gaia* being one of the names applied in Greek mythology to the living and life-giving Earth) in the late 1980s, and it is now accepted scientific theory.

He asserts: 'We define Earth as Gaia, because it presents itself as a complex entity embracing the biosphere, the atmosphere, the oceans and the land; in their totality, these elements constitute a cybernetic or self-sustaining system that provides an optimal physical and chemical medium for life on this planet.'[9]

This means that the concentration of gases in the atmosphere is fixed at a suitable level for living organisms. Any minor change could bring irreparable catastrophes. The level of oxygen in the atmosphere has remained unchanged, at around 21 per cent, for millions and millions of years. If it were to rise to 25 per cent there would be fires that would decimate the green covering of the earth's crust. The level of salt in the seas is of the order of 3.4 per cent. Were this to rise to 6 per cent, life in the seas would be impossible, as it is in the Dead Sea. This would unbalance the whole climatic system of the planet. And so on for all the remaining physical–chemical elements on the Mendeleiv scale.

Lovelock stresses: 'Life and its environment are so intrinsically interconnected that evolution applies to Gaia and not to organisms or their environment taken separately and on their own.'[10] This calibration is not simply internal to the Gaia-system, as though this were a closed system. It is verified in individual human beings, since our bodies contain more or less the same proportion of water as planet Earth (71%) and the same level of salinity in our blood as that of salt in the sea (3.4%), as Al Gore pointed out in his book on the balance of nature.[11]

Stephen Hawking, dealing with the origin and destiny of the universe in his famous *A Brief History of Time*, says: 'If the rate of expansion in the second immediately following the great explosion had been less, even in the proportion of just one in a hundred million trillion times, the universe would have exploded again before reaching its present size.'[12] And so there would be nothing of what there actually is. If, on the other hand, the explosion had been fractionally greater, to a tiny part per million, there would not have been sufficient density for the stars and planets to form and so for life to emerge. Everything happened in such a balanced way as to create conditions favourable for the possible emergence of life and consciousness. This what is called the 'soft' anthropic principle.[13]

The harmonious blending of the four basic interactions of the universe (gravitational, electro-magnetic, weak and strong nuclear) means that they continually work synergetically to keep the present cosmological arrow of time pointed to ever more related and complex forms of life. These, in effect, constitute the inner logic of the evolutionary process, the structure, so to speak – or perhaps rather the ordering 'Mind' – of the cosmos itself.[14] The Gaia system shows itself to be both extremely complex and ordered, which allows us to suppose that only a sovereign Intelligence would be capable of calibrating all these factors. Accepting such a fact is an act of reason and does not mean renouncing our own powers of reason. It does, though, mean humbly submitting to a higher and wiser Intelligence than our own.

III. The devastations suffered by Gaia

The Gaia hypothesis shows the robustness of Earth as a macro-organism in the face of the aggressions committed against its immune system. Throughout its long history, which now stretches back some 4.5 billion years, it has undergone various terrifying assaults.[15]

The great Cambrian extinction 570 million years ago caused the disappearance of 80–90 per cent of species then living. Then the Permo-Triassic extinction, 245 million years ago, probably the result of the super-continent Pangaea splitting in two, reduced existing species by some 75–95 per cent. In the Cretacean age, 67 million years ago, a meteor of huge proportions, thought to be about double the mass of Mount Everest, collided with Gaia, at a probable speed of 65 times the speed of sound. This caused the disappearance of 65 per cent of species then existing, notably the dinosaurs, which had lorded it over the earth for a hundred million years, but also marine plankton and innumerable other forms of life. Then in the Pleistocene epoch, 730,000 years ago, another massive cosmic event occurred, once again producing extinction of species on a huge scale. In a more recent period, the last ice age (between 15,000 and 10,000 B.C.), there was a mysterious huge devastation of species, this time sparing only Africa. It is estimated that 50 per cent of genera weighing more than five kilos vanished, along with 75 per cent of those weighing from 75 to 100 kilos, such as the mammoths, presumably as a result of climate changes associated with the irresponsible interventions of hunter-gatherer humans.[16]

Each time, whole banks of genetic coding, built up over millions and millions of years, were lost for ever. Scientists calculate, from the evidence of great mass extinctions, that such ecological disasters come about every 26 million years. Their origin would appear to lie in a hypothetical twin star to the Sun, known as Nemesis, some two to three light years away from us. This would cyclically draw the comets out of their normal orbits in the Oort cloud (a belt of comets and cosmic dust, identified by the Dutch astronomer Jan Oort; 1900–1992) and make them travel toward the Sun, with some of them colliding with Earth and thereby producing the destruction of large portions of the biosphere.[17]

Gaia had to re-adapt itself to the conditions left by each new assault and extinction; it regenerated its genetic stock from the survivals, created other durable species, and continued living, taking up the evolutionary process once more. The species existing today probably represent scarcely 1 per cent of the billions that have been on Earth since the emergence of life and were exterminated in the various catastrophes. At the present time, the excess of CFCs and other pollutants in the atmosphere, denounced by the IPCC (Intergovernmental Panel on Climate Change) in 2007, is possibly going to oblige the super-organism Earth to find new adaptations. These will not necessarily be favourable to the human species, the principal cause of global warming.

Some analysts indeed hold that the disappearance of species *homo* itself is a hypothesis that cannot be ruled out. Edward O. Wilson states that 'humankind is the first species in the history of life on Earth to have become a geophysical force' and that it is in the process of bringing about the sixth mass extinction.[18] Gaia would eliminate us in order to allow the global balance to persist and other species to live and so continue the cosmic course of evolution.[19] If Gaia has had to shed millions of species over the course of its history, who can guarantee that it will not be obliged to rid itself of ours, which has proved to be the Satan of Earth rather than its Good Angel? This is how I understand the warning by Théodore Monod, one of the last great modern naturalists: 'We are capable of senseless and demented behaviour; from now on, we can fear anything, including the annihilation of the human species; this would be a fair price for our lunacies and cruelties.'[20]

The well known economist-ecologist Nicolas Georgescu-Roegen suspects that, 'Perhaps the fate of human beings is to have a short but febrile life, exciting and extravagant, the opposite of a long, vegetative, and monotonous life. In this case, other species, lacking spiritual pretensions, such as amoebas, for example, will inherit an Earth that will still for a long time be bathed in the sun's light.'[21] Earth would be impoverished as a result, but – who knows? – perhaps millions and millions of years later, some new complex form of life (which Monod suggests might be a *cephalopod*, a sort of mollusc with a developed brain and a double memory) might bring the principle of intelligibility and loving-kindness back into the universe. New 'humans' would arise once more, perhaps with greater understanding of their cosmic and evolutionary mission within the universe and before the Creator. Earth would then have regained an evolutionary advance it had lost owing to the *hybris* (excessive arrogance) of the species *homo sapiens et demens*.

The Gaia hypothesis is highly plausible and is gaining increased consensus both within the scientific community and in cultural circles. It gives body to one of the most fascinating discoveries of the twentieth century, which is the deep complexity, unity, and harmony of the universe. It has become a splendid metaphor for a philosophical-religious vision underpinning ecological discourse.[22]

The new cosmology maintains that the universe is not made up of the sum total of its actual and possible beings but by the overall mass of webs of relationships among all beings, in such a way that one lives by another, for another, and with another: human beings are found to be a knot of relationships facing in all directions, rising up as an infinite project. Divinity itself is shown to be a pan-relational Reality.[23] If everything is relationship and nothing exists outside this relationship, then the most universal law is synergy, syntropy, inter-retro-relatedness, collaboration, cosmic solidarity, and universal brother/sisterhood.

This utopia of Gaia can re-enchant our manner of living together with Earth and make us practise an ethic of responsibility, of compassion and care, necessary attitudes at this time when the paradigm of civilization is changing.

IV. We are Earth that feels, loves, and venerates

Human beings, then, are the Earth itself at an advanced stage in its evolution, when it began consciously to feel, to think, to care, and to venerate. Earth is a generative principle. It represents the Mother who conceives, bears, and brings to light. In this way the archetype of Earth as Great Mother, Pachamama, or Grandmother emerges. In the same way that she generates everything and creates the right conditions for life, so she accepts everything and gathers everything into her bosom.[24]

Furthermore, Earth does not produce only us human beings. It produces the myriad micro-organisms that make up 90 per cent of the whole web of life and the insects that form the largest biomass in biodiversity.[25] It produces the waters, the green covering with its infinite variety of plants, flowers, and fruits. It produces the countless diversity of living creatures, animals, birds, and fishes, our companions in the sacred unity of life, since all carry the same basic genetic code: the twenty amino-acids and four phosphate bases. For all, it produces the conditions for evolution, subsistence, and nourishment, in the soil, the sub-soil, and the air. Feeling ourselves to be Earth is to merge into the terrestrial community, into the world of brothers and sisters, as exemplified by Francis of Assisi in his cosmic mysticism.

Each one of us needs to re-build this experience of radical communion with the Earth, in order to recover our earthly roots and nourish our own identity. A deep experience of Mother Earth will naturally give rise to experience of God as Mother of infinite tenderness and full of mercy. This experience, united to that of the Father of limitless love and goodness, will open us up to a more global and all-embracing experience of the mystery of God.

The collective consciousness is more and more widely coming to hold the view that Planet Earth is our Common Home, the only one we have to live in. It is therefore vital that we care for it, make it habitable for all, conserve it in its generosity, and preserve it in its integrity and splendour. This will give rise to a world *ethos* shared by all, capable of uniting human beings over and above their cultural differences, actually sensing ourselves to be sons and daughters of Earth who love and respect her as their own Mother.

Translated by Paul Burns

Notes

1. Cf. F. White, *The Overview Effect*, Boston: Houghton Mifflin, 1987.
2. *New York Times*, 9 Oct. 1982.
3. Cf. F. Capra and D. Steindal-Rast, *Pertenecendo ao universo*, São Paulo: Cultrix, 1993.
4. Cf. J. Gleick, *Chaos: Making a New Science*, New York: Penguin, 1988.
5. Cf. I. Progogine, *Order out of Chaos*, London: Heinemann, 1984.
6. Cf. J.-P. Dupuy, *Ordres et désordres. Essai sur un nouveau paradigme*, Paris: Seuil, 1992; P. R. Ehrlich, *The Machinery of Nature*, New York: Simon & Schuster, 1986.
7. Cf. E. Neuman and K. Kerény, *La Terra Madre e Dea. Sacralità della natura che ci fa vivere*, Como: Red Edizione, 1989.
8. Cf. J. E. Lovelock, *Gaia: A New Look at Life on Earth*, Oxford: Oxford University Press, 1987; *Ages of Gaia: A Biography of Our Living Earth*, Oxford: Oxford University Press; New York, W. W. Norton, 1988; *The Revenge of Gaia: Why the Earth is Hitting Back – and How We Can Still Save Humanity*, London and Santa Barbara, CA: Allen Lane, 2006.
9. Lovelock, *Gaia* p. 27.
10. Lovelock, *Ages of Gaia*, p. 17.
11. Al Gore, *Earth in the Balance: Finding a New Common Purpose*, London: Earthscan, 1992, p. 109.
12. S. Hawking, *A Brief History of Time*, London & New York: Bantam Dell, 1988, p. 172.
13. H. Küng, *Der Anfang aller Dinge. Naturwissenschaft und Religion*, Munich &

Zurich, Josef Piper, [7]2006 (Eng. trans. *The Beginning of All Things*, London: SCM Press, 2007, p. 147).

14. Cf. O. Goswami, *The Self-Aware Universe: How Consciousness Creates the Material World*, London & New York: Penguin, 1995.

15. P. Ward, *The End of Evolution. A Journey in Search of Clues to the Third Mass Extinction Facing Planet Earth*, New York: Bantam Books, 1995.

16. Data in B. Swimme and T. Berry, *The Universe Story: From the Primordial Flaring to the Ecozoic Era – A Celebrationof the Unfolding of the Cosmos*, San Francisco: HarperSanFrancisco, 1994, pp. 188–20. Also Z. Massoud, *Terre vivante*, Paris: Odile Jacob, 1992, pp. 27–30, 56.

17. E. O. Wilson, *The Future of Life*, New York: Knopf, 2002, pp. 33–47.

18. Wilson, *The Creation: An Appeal to Save Life on Earth*, New York, W. W. Norton, 2006, p. 38.

19. Cf. Lovelock, *Revenge of Gaia, op.cit.*

20. T. Monod, *Et si l'aventure humaine devait-elle échouer?*, Paris, Grasset, 2000, p. 246.

21. N. Georgescu-Roegen, *The Promethean Destiny*, New York: Penguin, 1987, p. 103.

22. Cf. R. Radford Ruether, *Gaia and God*, San Francisco: HarperSanFrancisco, 1992.

23. Cf. D. O'Murchu, *Evolutionary Faith: Rediscovering God in Our Great Story*, Maryknoll, NY: Orbis, 2002; D. Toolan, *At Home in the Cosmos*, Maryknoll, NY: Orbis, 2001.

24. E. Moltmann-Wendel, 'Gott und Gaia. Rückehr der Erde', *Evangelische Theologie 53*, Göttingen: Vanderhoek und Ruprecht, 1993, pp. 406–20; J. Moltmann, 'Die Erde und die Menschen. Zum theologischen Verständnis der Gaia-Hipothese', *ibid.*, pp. 420–30.

25. E. O. Wilson, *The Creation, op.cit*, p. 42.

2. Theology Responds to Earth

Ashes and Dust: On (not) Speaking about God Ecologically

ANNE ELVEY

On Monday 2 March 2009, like most if not all inhabitants of Victoria with mobile phones, I receive the following text message from the Victoria Police: 'Extreme weather expected tonight (Monday) & tomorrow. High wind & fire risk. Listen to the ABC local radio for emergency update. Do not reply to this message.' The following day the sky is overcast, a rarity in this summer and early autumn of ongoing drought in south-eastern Australia, and as I write I have one ear to any change in the wind. Even for those of us in the city, there is a sense of foreboding. Just over three weeks earlier, on a day that reached 46.4° Celsius in Melbourne, with a strong hot northerly wind that shifted toward the south as a cool change came late in the day, a firestorm broke upon towns in the bush to the north and east of the city. More than two hundred humans died and countless domestic animals and wild life. Tens of thousands of hectares of bush were burned. Some of the fires are still going as I write and friends in affected areas have had to decide whether to stay in their homes or retreat to the safety of the city.

Victoria is an Australian state most of whose citizens have their basic needs for food, water, shelter, health care, and education met, whose power supply is rarely interrupted, who are only just beginning to re-learn the lessons of restrained consumption that were routine for earlier settler, Depression, and post-war migrant generations, and many of whom have not learned the wisdom of Indigenous custodians of country. While we have registered the effects of climate change in floods in low-lying areas of Bangladesh, in the 2004 tsunami in south east Asia, in Hurricane Katrina in New Orleans, and in the rising sea levels already impacting on Pacific atolls such as Kiribati, for Victorians the devastating fires of 7 February 2009 are 'the face of climate change in our part of the world'.[1] Although there will be a Royal Commission into the causes of, and responses to, the fires, as Australian eco-philosopher Freya Mathews and many others have pointed out, two factors combined to produce environmental conditions for the massive fires. The land was desiccated due to lower rainfall over many years, and especially during January; a week of extreme heat, with maximum temperatures over 40° Celsius for several days, baked land and plants, causing native animals such as possums and bats to fall dead from their perches, and exotics, such as plane trees, to shed their leaves in a mock autumn.[2] These 'signs of the times' resonate with a 'knowing in our bones' that an increased frequency of extreme weather events can be expected as the 'new reality' of our climate.[3]

When climate change comes home to our own part of the world, we could interpret apocalyptically bats dropping, huddled families lost in an instant to a bushfire too swift to outrun, too intense to fight, and tough native vegetation half-dead above the cliff-tops on the Mornington Peninsula. Indeed the apocalyptic sensibility I bring even from my ecological, feminist, and, post-modern perspectives to my reading of the signs of climate change may be (unconsciously) informed by the apocalyptic breathings of the Bible.[4]

There is a level, too, at which the imminence of climate change places even the better-off of us in a situation closer to that of many of the biblical authors than we were for a while as we enjoyed our relative consumerist comfort and presumptions of human mastery of nature in a world we supposed to be without limits.[5] Even if we would now eschew the apocalyptic framework of much of the writing of the Jewish Second Temple period and the Christian second testament, the work of these texts (their writers and communities) to make meaning against the background of everyday struggle in dry landscape and subject to the forces of empire may open to us in a new way. In particular, the extremity of climate change suggests not so much that nature has become an enemy, but that we are confronted, as the biblical writers were before us, with a world of earth, air, fire, and water bigger than ourselves and our capacities for mastery. The opportunity for a revised understanding of ourselves as humans in a more than human Earth community raises particular questions concerning our thinking about the relation between humans and the 'more than' that we call God.

In a recent edition of *Concilium*, Erik Borgman writes: 'In its traditions, theology treasures ways of dealing with the incomprehensible, with the truth that is always withdrawing and never simply present.'[6] When in the face of anthropogenic climate change we endeavour to make meaning through theology, two intersecting questions present themselves: how are we to rethink the divine in the light of this new situation; what is an appropriate human response? When the other than human overwhelms us, we experience ourselves vulnerable, mortal, more aware of the fragility of our survival. In the case of the Victoria fires, the almost universal human response was characterised by empathy, compassion, generosity, and resilience, with a sense of connectedness not only to the human victims and survivors of the fires, but also to the other than human domestic and native animals affected. In the background of messages such as that sent by the Victoria Police is perhaps a new humility before the extremities of the weather. Moreover, with climate change, we live with a danger that remains. The disaster and the ongoing situation it signals remind us that we are not God or gods. But what, if anything, can we say of God?

Traditionally, Christian theologians have held together two modes of describing God: immanence and transcendence. On the whole, eco-theologies have favoured divine immanence – panentheist, rather than pantheist – that in a 'mutual indwelling' has God immanent in and embracing the more than human world, which includes humans.[7] With an emphasis less on divine presence in the cosmos than on the universe as present in God, Denis Edwards describes 'a panentheistic worldview, in which the Spirit can be thought of as 'making space' for an inter-related universe of creatures to evolve within the life of the divine Communion.'[8] To varying degrees ecological and related theologies hold together divine immanence and divine transcendence, valuing Earth and cosmos as divinely infused, while not constraining God or the operation of grace to the limits of any particular human world.[9] While these approaches offer much for an eco-theology, the extremity of climate change challenges even panentheistic concepts that hold together divine immanence, divine transcendence, and the immanence of Earth and cosmos in God. Where is God in, or in relation to, a firestorm that destroys both native and feral animals, their immediate ecosystems, humans, houses, cattle and sheep, horses and crops, and companion animals?

Possible responses to this question include:

1. God is not in the firestorm; rather God transcends the Earthly unfolding of more than human (including human) activity; God's agency in the firestorm is simply that agency of a natural order obedient to, or unfolding according to, its divinely-ordained innate laws and processes.
2. God is in the firestorm; through the incarnation, God is intimately en-mattered with all things, tied to their processes in all their energetic, chaotic, and consequential unfolding.

3. As a consequence of human action (anthropogenic climate change and in
    some instances arson) and more than human conditions (the fuel load in
    the forests, drought, heat, and winds), the firestorm represents a judg-
    ment on human action, in which God and a more than human Earth
    community are co-agents.
4. God is not so much in the firestorm as in the human response of compas-
    sion toward its victims and survivors, in their grace and resilience in loss,
    and in the works of mourning and beginning again.
5. God is in the land, animals, and people seared by the firestorm; God
    suffers and grieves with its victims and survivors.

While each of these responses resonates with some aspects of biblical
theology, I want to suggest that from an ecological perspective, we need to
begin the exploration of God-talk elsewhere, to start with what Deborah
Rose, following Emil Fackenheim, writes of as a 'turning toward' our here
and now, with the resonance of the *metanoia* we find in the Gospel of Mark
(1.15) and in the late Pope John Paul II's appeal to an 'ecological conversion'[10]
Arguing that in Australia we live in colonized space, Rose writes: 'In space
that is fragmented, in places that are broken, in the knowledge that much
damage is not even visible, only certain kinds of actions are ethically possible'.[11] In such a space, 'turning toward' is 'based on dialogue; that is, on the
exchange of knowledge and care among persons' and 'must begin where one
is'.[12] It requires us 'to bear the burden of our history, and at the same time to
act with hope'.[13] Rose reminds us that this hope must be realistic, not based
in myths of 'conquest or seduction' where a desire for wholeness turns from
the ruptures of the here and now, appealing for example to a romanticised
other (the noble savage, the pristine wilderness), an ideal home, an idyllic
past (a paradise lost), or 'golden' future (an earthly haven, an otherworldly
heaven).[14] Rather 'turning toward' is an ethical process of engagement in the
fracture of the here and now.

If we orient this 'turning toward' to the more than human community of
Earth, especially in the particularity of climate change (a global phenomenon
with particular effects in place), we cannot begin with Christian theologies.
We need to assent first to our here and now, not passively, but as the situation
of ecological (including social) fragmentation in which we find ourselves
and are actively engaged. We need to take the risk that if we attend to Earth
as a more than human constituency of organic, inorganic, material others
– which are variously mineral, leafy, watery, gassy, bacterial, viral, corporeal,
inter-related; which run, chirp, speak, write, build, eat, compose and decom-

pose; and which respond to heat, cold, light, shade, darkness, proximity, distance, sound, touch, and relationship in particular ways – then we must put aside our religious understandings. By putting aside, I do not mean that we deny or ignore them, but in the mode of the mystic set them aside, allowing that what is needful in them will be safe in the interim. Rather than putting one's understanding aside 'to strive upward . . . toward a union with him [*sic*] who is beyond all being and knowledge', we need to redirect the kenotic orientation of mystical practice toward our more than human context, allowing what we know of God and the Earth community to rest in a 'cloud of forgetting'.[15] In such a practice, attention to our more than human here and now is not a hindrance to openness to God, but its only precondition.

What is required is a letting go of what we think we know of God and ourselves, in particular, easy understandings of God as creator and ourselves and the Earth that is our home as creation. We need not to assume that we know the Earth story, neither the stories of Genesis 1 and 2 or Proverbs 8, nor the new cosmology that has become so popular in some eco-spiritual circles.[16] At the same time, we need to put aside our certainty that when we hold a handful of soil we know what it is we are holding. Taking as a paradigm an approach that lets God be beyond our understanding and rests in openness to what we do not know of God, to God's alterity, we need to turn toward Earth with the same attitude of openness to the other's being. But we need also to remember that this other is of a particular kind, it is another of which we are ourselves part, and that in opening to an Earthly otherness we recognize an otherness in ourselves.

All this needs to happen with a quality of reverence that does not assume that Earth is either divine or not divine. Rather moving beyond a matter/ spirit split, the materiality of Earth is already the locus of its transcendence. I have suggested elsewhere that we think in terms of a material transcendence.[17] This has problems insofar as the concept of a material transcendence seems to reverse the spirit/matter dualism by shifting the focus to the previously devalued term 'matter'. While this may be the case, and ideally I would speak of a materially spiritual, spiritually material transcendence, the shift of focus is important. Generally, the material has at worst been represented as non-spiritual, even anti-spiritual, at best as the *locus* of divine immanence, so to put together material and transcendence is to return a certain respect, for matter's inherent otherness and spiritual non-negotiability, to the material.

However, there is a further problem with a material transcendence. A firestorm so clearly transcends human and other corporeal beings. Even where, as a mechanism for rendering viable certain seeds, fire may enable the later burgeoning of new floral life, a firestorm destroys whole habitats. In the face of its terrifying otherness, openness to a material transcendence cannot be understood as the kind of openness that simply welcomes the other. Rather, if a material transcendence is to remain useful as a concept for rethinking our ethical relationship with more than human others, an openness to the alterity of the other needs to be understood as an orientation to learning from the other of its being, which may call forth variously welcome, compassion, wonder, solidarity, prudence, and resistance. But is this enough?

The overwhelming character and effects of the firestorm are reminding us of a 'more than' that is materially other and not comfortably accommodated to notions of divine immanence or divine judgment. It may be easier to understand God as outside the fire, either as a prior creator who lets things be, or in the suffering people, animals, places affected by the fire, or in responses of compassion and graceful resilience. But this leaves us somewhat arbitrarily deciding that God is immanent only in some aspects of the materiality of our here and now. Perhaps 'where is God?' or even 'what kind of God?' are not the best questions to be asking.

Like the firestorm, the idea of God reminds us that we are not masters. However, too often in the idea of God, human mastery has been replaced by a divine mastery that becomes a warrant for reinstating master/slave dynamics, especially in the relationship between elite humans and Earth others. In a time of climate change, the assumption that the effects of living with the land, however benignly, are under our control replays the illusion of mastery. But substituting a divine master for human ones is inadequate. The gift – if such a word can be used, and I use it advisedly with all the nuances of gift and poison to which Jacques Derrida alerts us[18] – of both the idea of God and the reality of the firestorm is the possibility of a re-learning of humility before the other.[19] In this time of ongoing ecological crisis, a new humility, with its resonances of humus and humanness, may be the human vocation.

Humility may mean that speaking about God entails not speaking about God. Learning humility is about learning who we are in the more than human world that is our community and habitat. Learning humility is about learning what we are not: neither God nor gods, and perhaps not even very good ecologists. In the wake of the firestorm, we hear 'we must rebuild'; but humility means listening to the charred place. Is it time to rebuild? Does the soil need to rest from human habitation? Are there toxins melted into its layers that need to be removed? Does the land itself need time to mourn? In the wake of the firestorm, when we respond to the ones made homeless by the fires, humility reminds us that we do not always recognize our neighbours so readily. Through climate change many are or will become homeless beyond our borders.

Humility invites us to mourn. When we mourn we acknowledge that what we have loved is not in our power to keep. Humility invites us to open ourselves to the material/corporeal reality of loss in which we find ourselves still alive and sustained as humans interrelated with humus, especially when in the days following the fires as smoke hung in the air over Melbourne, we literally breathed the losses. On the day of mourning for victims of the firestorm, the Governor General of Australia, Quentin Bryce, said:

> The unthinkable, we must think. The unimaginable, we must see. The unspeakable, we must speak. The unbearable, we must weep.
>
> We must allow the thoughts and images and words that have so recently scorched and swamped us to gently settle, and find their proper and worthy place in our hearts and minds.
>
> We must recognize these memories as an inseparable part of us. They are the makeup of our growing wisdom and our fresh intent. We are altered by them, yet they are what will forever sustain us.[20]

Humility takes us to the edge of what it is to be human, reminding us both of our extraordinary resilience and open-heartedness and of their limits. It is a kind of kenosis, which has theological import in terms of its capacity to turn us toward the reality of our situation. However much we eschew notions of truth, as they suggest mastery, this humble openness to what is, allows a reappropriation of the idea of truth. Borgman writes: 'The Truth is present in our day and age as the kenotic awareness that however much we know, reveal and comprehend of reality, its hiddenness and incomprehensibility are always bigger.'[21]

A humble turning toward our more than human here and now does not entail an ethics of passivity before the surfeit of the other, but an acting *with* the world as we find it, allowing the more than human world 'to change itself'.[22] This approach resonates with the work of poets who bring into their craft an attentiveness to the more than human; writing with, rather than on behalf of, the other; understanding the craft of writing as an expression of their embeddedness in their here and now.[23] Kevin Hart comments: 'It has become common for many of our best poets to confine themselves to elevating the mind to sacred things without actually affirming them.'[24] In some cases, this phenomenon may represent the kind of religious kenosis I am suggesting, where an attentiveness to our more than human here and now is accompanied by a putting aside of God-talk. Two examples come to mind. Ellen Bass's poem 'If There Is No God' lovingly evokes a more than human world, suggesting that the human vocation is not so much to rely on a divine saviour as to love something 'enough to watch over' it.[25] Chris Wallace-Crabbe's 'Glory Be' focuses on insects in their habitats, beginning with the absence of dragonflies and ending with their presence at Wye River, at which point he redirects Gerard Manley Hopkins' 'God's Grandeur'; not vanished, the dragonflies are

> glinting with what could be God's grandeur,
> in a certain, maybe natural frame of things.[26]

Significantly, in both instances, the putting aside of God-talk retains reference to God. A religious kenosis oriented toward our more than human context carries the tone of an apophatic (or negative) theology. Such apophasis always retains traces not only of that to which it is oriented in unknowing but also of that which is set aside in an active forgetting. In the case of a humble turning toward the more than human that delights and terrifies, sustains and destroys, and is a space of possibility and limit, the idea of God remains. The 'more than' of God opens a space for understanding ourselves, and responding, in a more than human network of relationships and challenges that can overwhelm us. Can we recover a divine 'more than' that is non-identical with the 'more than' of fire and climate change, but at the same time interconnected with the wider 'more than' of the Earth community in indefinable ways that can shift our anthropocentric focus? The human vocation to humility, a vocation to turn toward the fragmentation of our here and now, can be also a vocation to be open to something that Christians have called grace, but a grace grounded in the material. Our terror of the Victoria fires of 7 February 2009 has its own grace, not only in the response of human compassion but also in the new situation in which we find ourselves pressed to attend more humbly to weather and wind in a way that many urban Australians had forgotten.

Notes

1. Freya Mathews, 'The Deadly Inevitability of Climate Change', *The Age*, 10 Feb. 2009, http://www.theage.com.au/opinion/fires-the-deadly-inevitability-of-climate-change-20090209-8289.html?page=-1, accessed 1 Mar. 2003.
2. Mathews, 'The Deadly Inevitability of Climate Change'.
3. *Ibid.*.

4. See Catherine Keller, *Apocalypse Now and Then: A Feminist Guide to the End of the World*, Boston: Beacon Press, 1996.

5. On the illusion of a world without limits see Garrett Hardin, 'Ecology and the Death of Providence', *Zygon* 15, 1 (1980): 57–8. For a critique of a logic of human mastery of nature, see Val Plumwood, *Feminism and the Mastery of Nature*, London: Routledge, 1993.

6. Erik Borgman, 'Theology: Discipline at the Limits', *Concilium* 2006/2: pp. 141–51.

7. On panentheism see, *e,g*, for example, Elizabeth A. Johnson, *Women, Earth and Creator Spirit*, New York: Paulist Press, 1993, pp. 42–3; see also Sallie McFague's description of the world as the body of God: Sallie McFague, *The Body of God: An Ecological Theology*, Minneapolis: Fortress Press, 1993, pp. 191–5.

8. Denis Edwards, *Breath of Life: A Theology of the Creator Spirit*, Maryknoll, NY: Orbis Books, 2004, p. 2; see also pp. 130–42.

9. See, for example, Rosemary Radford Ruether, 'The God of Possibilities: Immanence and Transcendence Rethought', *Concilium* 2000/4: pp. 45–54.

10. Deborah Bird Rose, 'Rupture and the Ethics of Care in Colonized Space', in Tim Bonyhady and Tom Griffiths (eds), *Prehistory to Politics: Humanities and the Public Intellectual*, Carlton South, Vic.: Melbourne University Press, 1996, pp. 190–215, esp. 215; see also Emil Fackenheim, *To Mend the World: Foundations of Post-Holocaust Jewish Thought*, Bloomington: Indiana University Press, 1994. On 'ecological conversion' see John Paul II, 'General Audience, Wednesday 17 January 2001', para. 4, http://www.vatican.va/holy_father/john_paul_ii/audiences/2001/documents/hf_jp-ii_aud_20010117_en.html, accessed 12 Mar. 2009; also, Barry Blundell, 'Editorial: The call to ecological conversion', *Compass: A Review of Topical Theology* 37, Autumn 2003, http://www.compassreview.org/autumn03/1.html, accessed 12 Mar. 2009.

11. Rose, 'Rupture and the Ethics of Care', 214.

12. *Ibid.*

13. *Ibid.*

14. *Ibid.*, pp. 208–13.

15. Cf. Pseudo-Dionysius, 'The Mystical Theology', in Pseudo-Dionysius, *The Complete Works*, trans. Colm Luibheid, London: SPCK, 1987, pp. 133–41, esp. p. 133; Anonymous, *The Cloud of Unknowing*, in *The Cloud of Unknowing and The Book of Privy Counselling*, ed. William Johnston, New York: Doubleday, 1973, pp. 53–4.

16. Particularly influential in Australia has been the work of Thomas Berry and Brianne Swimme, *e.g.*, their *The Universe Story: From the Primordial Flaring Forth to the Ecozoic Era – a Celebration of the Unfolding of the Cosmos*, San Francisco: HarperSan Francisco, '1992.

17. See Anne Elvey, 'Material Elements: The Matter of Women, the Matter of Earth, the Matter of God', in Lisa Isherwood and Kathleen McPhillips (eds),

Anne Elvey

Post-Christian Feminisms: A Critical Approach, Aldershot: Ashgate, 2008, pp. 53–69.

18. Jacques Derrida, *Glas*, trans. John P. Leavey and Richard Rand, Lincoln: University of Nebraska Press, 1986, p. 116.

19. See Lisa Gerber, 'Standing Humbly before Nature', *Ethics and the Environment* 7, 1 (2002): 39–53.

20. Ms Quentin Bryce, AC, Governor-General of the Commonwealth of Australia, 'Address at the National Memorial Service for the Victorian Bushfire Victims', Rod Laver Arena, Melbourne, 22 Feb. 2009, http://www.gg.gov.au/governorgeneral/speech.php?id=522; accessed 11 March 2009.

21. Borgman, 'Theology', *art. cit.*, p. 147.

22. See Freya Mathews, 'Letting the World Do the Doing', *Australian Humanities Review* 33 (Aug.-Oct. 2004), http://www.australianhumanitiesreview.org/archive/Issue-August-2004/matthews.html, accessed 12 Mar. 2009.

23. For more sustained reflection on the problems and possibilities of writing with the more than human, see Kate Rigby, 'Earth, World, Text: On the (Im)Possibility of Ecopoiesis', *New Literary History* 35 (2004): 427–42, and her 'Writing after Nature', *Australian Humanities Review* 39–40 (2006), http://www.australianhumanitiesreview.org/archive/Issue-September-2006/rigby.html, accessed 5 November 2007.

24. Kevin Hart, 'Poetry and Revelation: Hopkins, Counter-Experience and Reductio', *Pacifica: Australasian Theological Studies* 18, 3 (2005): 259–80, see 267.

25. Ellen Bass, 'If There Is No God', *Women's Studies Quarterly* 2001, 1 & 2: 194–5.

26. Chris Wallace-Crabbe, 'Glory Be', *Island* 114 (Spring 2008): 68–9.

Toward an Inter-religious Eco-theology

FELIX WILFRED

'Before we knew where the gods were. They were in the trees. Now there are no more trees'
– The Raji people inhabiting the border between India and Nepal[1]

'I said to the almond tree, 'Sister, speak to me of God,'
and the almond tree blossomed'
– Nikos Kazantzakis [2]

The crisis of the earth becomes also a crisis of God and a crisis of human beings when nature stops being a manifestation of the divine. If crisis is an opportunity for rethinking and change, then we need to look at the inter-relationship of religions vis-à-vis the unprecedented crisis that afflicts our earth. We require the concerted effort of all religious traditions to respond to the ecological crisis, each one drawing out the best of its resources. Construction of a common eco-theology by the various faiths could con-tribute to the transformation of consciousness, attitudes, and a new praxis in relation to the earth. Here we have an opportunity to forget the past and forge unity. While our understanding of God and human beings continues to divide religions, it is less likely that the earth will divide them. On the contrary, today it is the earth that holds the prospect of bringing the religions together and so leading them to a meaningful dialogue on God and human-ity. The horizon of our understanding of human beings, of creation, and of God will be widened through a continuing dialogue focused on nature and the environment.

I. Evolution – a common point of reference

The inter-religious eco-theology I am envisaging is one that will be based on solid empirical data provided by science. For this we need to have a more dynamic understanding of and approach to nature as furnished by scientific

43

facts. The development of a more complex and evolutionary understanding of nature would be of fundamental importance. The inter-dependence and inter-connectedness of reality take on specificity if we adopt an evolutionary perspective. Biological evolution tells us that no species is independent or self-enclosed or static but has undergone mutation and development. It helps us overcome the walls that separate the various species in nature and see them sharing many things in common, including ancestry, genetic code, and the process of germination of life, its growth and flourishing, decay and dissolution. Humans are no exceptions to these, but rather form part of these primordial realities of life-processes. In this way, biological science reinforces our understanding of relationality in the universe and helps us view human beings themselves from this larger frame of reference.

Interdependence in terms of the 'origins of species' and similarity in terms of life-processes, however, does not rule out the obvious presence of conflict in nature –which many see as scandalous – and any organic and holistic view that ignores this would be too idyllic. Ultimately, the evolutionary perspective helps us overcome nature-destroying anthropocentrism by making us aware that human beings are one species among many, and it reinforces the inter-connectedness of the entire creation and the need for a holistic understanding. In particular, it makes us realize how much we humans are part of an interlocking eco-system and how we depend on the elements of the universe – the earth, air, water, fire, and the sky, what the Hindu tradition calls the *'panchabhuta'*, for our very existence.[3]

What is special about the evolutionary perspective of nature is not that it is science but that it is a *different science* from the mechanistic one, especially in its technological application. The evolutionary perspective seems to intersect with the fundamental *weltanschauung* of Hinduism, Buddhism, Daoism, etc. For monotheistic religious traditions, reconciling themselves with this perspective has been problematic, as shown by the long opposition to evolution in the Christian tradition, which even today is still widespread.

II. Eco-theology – an inter-religious project

An evolutionary framework is very important for any inter-religious eco-theology. In some of the religious traditions, such as like Hinduism, Buddhism, and Daoism, evolutionary thought is interwoven into their beliefs and world-views, while other traditions, such as Christianity, Judaism, and Islam, may have a more static view of nature, earth, and the universe. Therefore, what is called for is a convergence of all religious traditions. In any case, scientific evolutionism challenges all religions – albeit in different grades – and their attitudes toward the earth and all forms of life. Indigenous and primeval religious traditions, rather than being doctrines and beliefs, tend to embody the relationship of peoples to the ecosystem in their day-to-day expressions, and they are repositories also of the indigenous knowledge and classification of the biodiversity of the region.

The common responsibility of religions toward the earth would call for a re-examination and re-interpretation of some of their foundational conceptions regarding God, human beings, and nature. 'As we confront the environmental crisis, all religious traditions, if they are to survive and continue to contribute to solutions, must undergo some degree, perhaps a considerable degree, of reconstruction. Such work cannot be undertaken without a thorough and courageous examination of foundations. To list, marshal, or even carefully orchestrate apparently eco-friendly elements of any religious traditions and then declare the whole tradition ecologically sound, without having critically examined the deeper context, will produce short-lived inspiration at best.'[4]

In recent times there have been attempts in the Christian tradition to interpret the mystery of God, of Christ, and of faith in general from an evolutionary perspective, thereby bringing Christian beliefs closer to nature and its processes. By way of example we may think of the reflections of Karl Rahner on Christology and of Piet Schoonenberg on creation.[5] But now what is called for is for us to re-think our relationship to the earth in a more fundamental way, from the evolutionary perspective as well as from what Hinduism, Buddhism, Daoism, Confucianism and so on offer in this regard. They try to explicate the human starting from the universe and not the other way round as is done in anthropocentric approaches. This is important, since our relationship to earth has serious practical implications. We cannot remain simply at the level of explaining traditional doctrines from an evolutionary perspective: we also need to see what kind of praxis and attitudes they imply.

An unenlightened labelling of traditions such as Hinduism as being monistic and pantheistic prevented Christianity from taking up the deeper insights and challenges these traditions presented.[6] Christian tradition needs to develop more and more the immanent dimension of the Divine mystery, which is a necessary prelude to a deeper and meaningful understanding of nature and the earth. Therefore, the experience of seeing God in everything, which is also part of the Christian mystical tradition, needs to be fostered. This provides a point of intersection with Hinduism and other

Eastern traditions. We need to reopen the question of salvation in dialogue with them, and indeed in a more radical and transformative way.

III. Partners in the salvation of *terra mater* and the human species

Not long ago a question that seriously agitated many theological minds was whether non-Christians possess elements of salvation for humanity. Today, we should respond by saying that other religious traditions have crucial and indispensable vision and values for the salvation of the earth without which there will be no salvation and future for humanity. Therefore, the new question that we need to pose is: What can Christianity learn in dialogue with other religious traditions for the salvation of the planet Earth so that human salvation can happen? A deeper dialogue will lead to the evolving of an inter-religious eco-theology.

The convergence of perspectives among religions and a common engagement in the cause of the environment and social justice will naturally lead them to challenge the present dominant economy. In this sense, religions necessarily have to become political for the salvation of humanity. A greed- and competition-based system of economy and an unbridled production and consumption pattern will stretch the earth beyond its regenerative capacity. Unchecked, this system and pattern of life will lead the human species to disaster and even extinction. That will be the revenge of nature, which will go on even without the human species. If not here, where does the discourse of salvation, of such concern to all religions, begin?

Where there is greed, instrumentalization is also inevitably at work. Instrumentalization of the earth goes along with manipulation of human beings and negation of equity through a play of power and domination. These are diametrically opposed to salvation, which is a reality beyond teleology. From this perspective the earth and nature are to be respected in themselves and not to be viewed simply as objects for the fulfilment of human greed. The earth has its own rhythm as a mother carrying all beings in its womb and caring for them. Efforts such as the creation of nature parks, animal conservation projects, and the like are technical solutions that do not measure up to the moral and spiritual crisis stemming from the greedy and wasteful use of natural resources. They seem to separate the realm of facts from those of values. We need to hold these together in responding to the ecological crisis. As the 'love of money is the root of all evil' (1 Tim 6.10), so is greed at the root of the ecological crisis. The radical solution will appear when we address the issue of greed interwoven with violence and aggression of all kinds, and it is again here that we need to look to the religious traditions for their wisdom and insights, and especially when they jointly develop inter-religious perspectives on such fundamental issues, which conjoin facts and values. Such a common engagement cannot but revitalize religions and their theologies, which will also gain in credibility. As the Dalai Lama notes with reference to his Buddhist tradition, 'In Buddhist practice we get so used to this idea of non-violence and the ending of all suffering that we become accustomed to not harming or destroying anything indiscriminately. Although one does not believe that trees or flowers have minds, we treat them with respect. Thus, we share a sense of universal responsibility for both mankind and nature.'[7]

The way we live in relation to nature also shows whether we are violent or non-violent. Non-violent and compassionate behaviour is reflected in the way people approach nature and all the materials things of daily life – either wantonly and aggressively destroying them or nurturing and caring for them. Inter-religious eco-theology will seek to imbue our approach to nature with a sense of sacredness (which is not to be confused with 'sacralization of nature') and a sense of wonder and mystery. To put it in Christian theological terminology, this could be called a sacramental approach to creation, which will help us to correct and balance an overly anthropocentric approach with a lot of emphasis on time and history. The realization and experience of the immanent presence of the Spirit in all of creation helps us overcome the gulf that in traditional understanding divides the creator from and the created universe:[8]

> Nature speaks a truth scarcely heard and, up until recent years, insufficiently formulated among theologians. In our minds, we have eliminated or excluded the role of created nature as central to the salvation of the world. I say 'in our minds' advisedly, because if God is revealed in the created world, then God is present 'in all things' (Col. 3.11). In other words, there is an invisible dimension to all things visible, a 'beyond' to everything material. All creation is a palpable mystery, an immense 'incarnation' of cosmic proportions.[9]

IV. The burden of the past

Religions cannot play their role in overcoming ecological crisis as unblemished contributors, for they have been responsible in various ways for the negative attitude to nature and have been ideological partners in the exploitation of nature. This exploitation, as eco-feminists tell us, is associated with domination over women. Therefore, like evolutionism, eco-feminism too needs to be drawn into the inter-religious eco-theological project, because of the important contribution it could make. While patriarchy dominates nature, eco-feminism gives central importance to care and nurturing and to the connectedness of the whole of reality beyond the dualism of matter/ spirit, body/soul, male/female, etc.[10]

Think of the very distinction in the Christian theological tradition between the natural and the supernatural: this implies a devaluation of the natural, as if salvation consists in moving away from what is natural. We cannot expect this premise to produce a positive outlook on nature or the earth, or any help in overcoming the ecological crisis. On the whole, the same body/soul dualism that created a prejudicial attitude and praxis toward women has been sanctioned by religions in regard to nature as well.

The ascetic ideals and spirituality religious traditions have developed, each in its own way, have been far from sympathetic to nature and its elements. Hinduism and Buddhism may not have taught dominion of human beings over the earth, but they have in them certain ascetic ideals that foster disconnection and flight from the world and nature, causing a rift and dualism. Even well-meant efforts to interpret Christian faith in an evolutionary framework (meaning a matter-spirit continuum) have not been able to hide dualism and hierarchization, as, for example, when spirit is said to be, in Karl Rahner's view, a self-transcendence of matter. '[W]e then must . . . try to see man [*sic*] as the being in whom the basic tendency of matter to find itself in the spirit by self-transcendence arrives at the point where it definitely breaks through; thus in this way we may be in a position to regard man's being itself, from this view-point within the basic and total conception of the world.'[11]

Matter has its own consistency, and its reality is not to be judged in what it is in relationship to the spirit as the teleological goal of matter itself. Is the future of the universe going to be a transformation of all matter into spirit? What then will happen to our earth with all its materiality?

V. A reappraisal

A second aspect we need to consider is that of the relationship between creation and the mystery of God. In the Semitic or monotheistic religious traditions the relationship between the creation and the creature is viewed through causality. So the Psalmist could say, 'The heavens are telling the glory of God; and the firmament proclaims his handiwork' (Ps. 19.1). Both are differentiated and clearly demarcated with God as the cause and creation as the marvellous effect. In Hindu tradition the world and God are not two different realities. From the perspective of *advaita* (non-dual) thought, God and world are viewed neither as a single reality nor as two separate entities. This has led to an outlook, attitude, and praxis that – in a weaker sense – presuppose an immanent divine presence in nature or – in a stronger sense – see the whole universe as the body of God. These intuitions have found poetic, mythical, devotional, and ritual expressions in the Hindu tradition over millennia. Expressing the basic Hindu intuition in an aesthetic image, I would say that the relationship of the creator to creation is that of a dancer becoming the dance itself. In fact, in Hindu Saivite tradition, Siva creates the whole universe through his eternal dance. The motion and rhythm of the divine dance keep the entire universe in movement.

Buddhism, for its part, would challenge the very category of causality at the basis of the differentiation between creator and creation. It speaks of 'dependent co-origination' (*pratityasamutpada*) of the whole of reality, which allows no room for the idea of cause and effect. On the contrary, the cause is in the effect, as much as the effect is in the cause, something that helps us to interpret the divine immanence in a much more intense and deeper way than a perspective of hierarchization of cause and effect as found in the traditional interpretation of the relationship between creator and creation.

The close relationship with nature is very characteristic of the Chinese vision of Daoism too. It views virtue in the human realm as the reflection of the healthy principles of balance and systemic equilibrium at work in nature. The health of the human body itself is a situation of homeostasis in which the principles of *yin* and *yang* are correlated and balanced and the body in turn is in tune with the environment. Hence harmony with nature is commended as the way we need to follow for our general well-being of mind and body. How could one dismiss this whole beautiful vision as simply 'natural' and view human salvation as something super-natural? But, on the other hand, does not a deeper Christian intuition see the body itself as the hinge of salvation – *caro cardo salutis?*

VI. Is Christianity to blame?

Lynn White's well-known critique, laying the blame for the ecological crisis at the door of Christianity, is somewhat simplistic as it fails to make necessary distinctions and differentiations.[12] Provoked by this thesis, biblical scholars have tried to interpret dominion as stewardship, care, and so on. I do not think these exegetical exercises take us far. There is the incontrovertible evidence of the consequences of an approach that actually shows domination as the way biblical tradition has been interpreted in praxis. But the point is that this domination and mastery are something for which Christianity in its entirety is not to be blamed. The Oriental and Orthodox traditions show a much more earth-related understanding of faith and creation.

The truth is that the Christianity that is blamed is a Christianity interpreted through the enlightenment anthropocentrism of the West, which fostered disenchantment with nature as a mark of progress and of secular humanism. Christianity and Christian heritage were one-sidedly interpreted to produce the project of the Western Enlightenment and were in turn profoundly influenced by it. This same Enlightenment taught that creativity in human beings emerges by transcending, through freedom, the world of nature or the realm of necessity. A misinterpretation of Genesis 1.28 in favour of human sovereignty served the anthropocentric purposes of the Enlightenment. Therefore, the project of inter-religious eco-theology, which will bring Christianity into dialogue with other religious traditions, may help it recover the hidden dimension of its ecological message and provide an occasion to bring to light the ecological sensitivity we find in the Christian tradition as borne out in the life of St Francis of Assisi, Hildegard of Bingen, and others.

VII. Reinterpreting tradition

The factors that are responsible for anti-ecological attitudes must also include the role played by what I would call *an inflated historical consciousness* in Christian tradition. The practice of domination goes hand in hand with an exaggerated historical consciousness, seeing human beings as the master-interveners who re-create the world and the order of the earth in their image through the exercise of their freedom. Concepts of millennium and apocalypticism are closely tied to this outlook and conception of history.

The projection of this perspective has overshadowed the biblical conception of a cyclical renewal, which is closer to the rhythm of nature. Six days of work are followed by a break or the leisure of the Sabbath, and so it continues. Similarly every six years of cultivation are followed by a pause, leaving the land fallow to renew its energies. And then there is the cycle of Jubilee by which the relationship of humans to the land is re-ordered. This renews both the earth and human society.

These are perspectives that will help us forge closer relationships with Oriental religions and echo their view of nature, land, and human society. They therefore need to be highlighted in Christian theological reflection, which has unfortunately tended over the past two hundred years to support human history and its domination as supreme values, forgetful of our responsibility to the earth and of the respect we owe to the rhythm of the earth that continues to nourish us. This relationship to the earth facilitates the realization of the divine immanence, as when Paul says 'In him we live and move and have our being' (Acts 17.28). This immanence relates not only to human beings but to the entire cosmos. We understand more closely what 'God all in all' means (cf. 1 Cor. 15.28) when Dionysius the Areopagite, from his typical mystical perspective, tells us that 'while remaining within God's self, God is also in the world (*encosmic*), around the world (*pericosmic*) and above the world (*hypercosmic*), that God is above heaven, and above all being, that God is sun, star and fire, water, wind and dew, cloud, archetypal stone and rock, that God is all, that God is no thing'.[13] Such a Christian reinterpretation of creator and the created in terms of immanence will interlock with the vision of many of the other religious traditions of the world, especially with Hinduism. There is then a lot of scope for an appropriate inter-religious eco-theology for today.

VIII. Eco-theology in practice

Gandhi did not use any environmental rhetoric current today, nor did he romanticize nature. Unlike his contemporary, the poet Tagore, Gandhi rarely spoke of trees, birds, animals, landscapes, rivers, or mountains. Abstemious though he was, at first sight there is nothing that could quality him as an environmentalist; nothing that could inspire us ecologically. But this would be mistaken. His whole way of life reveals an *embedded ecotheology*. He was opposed to wasting nature's resources and to anything that would upset the balance of the natural environment. Voluntary restraint from use of things beyond the minimum required fosters the resources of nature.

Gandhi's entire life functioned much like an ecosystem. This was one life in which every least act, emotion, or thought had its place: the succinctness of Gandhi's enormous written output, his small meals of nuts and fruits, his morning ablution and everyday bodily practices, his periodic observance of silence, his morning walks, his cultivation of the small as much as of the big, his abhorrence of waste, his resort to fasting – all these point to the manner in which the symphony was orchestrated.[14]

The critical question is how such individual practices can bring about the kind of structural change we require. But that is not to undermine the value of restraint and renunciation translated in practice, meaning frugal use of natural resources. The point is that we need to create an environment and structures that would encourage more and more people and groups to espouse similar practices. Like voluntary silence, which conserves human energy, frugal use of the goods of the earth helps to preserve the equilibrium of nature. It has its social implications in as much as it contributes to creating equitable social relationships. Here we understand both the implications of a theology that inextricably links the creator to the created and the bonds that bind human beings to the earth.

What many environmentalists fail to acknowledge is that there is a deep co-relation between our approach to nature and the kind of relationship prevailing in society. The destruction of the ecosystem at the same time causes wounds of injustice in the body of society. Inter-religious eco-theology then should lead us logically to joint engagement in the question of social justice. An equitable distribution of natural resources is the best guarantee against the exploitative use of them that is causing the present environmental crisis.

A religiously-inspired approach to nature and its protection can succeed where appeals to reason seem to fail. In fact the movement for recovery of nature in the West has recently been employing the religious symbolism of *Gaia* – the earth-goddess.[15] I should like to highlight here that the *Chipko* movement in India – one of the largest ecological movements in the world – was religiously inspired, and it affirms the spiritual value of nature. Women of the Himalaya region in North India were involved in protecting the trees of their villages when economic interests sought to fell the forests, and they hugged these trees, preventing them from being felled. There are numerous such examples from indigenous peoples all over the world: their approach to nature offers a lot of insights for an eco-theology.[16]

Conclusion

There is a growing realization that we need a change of paradigm in our relationship to nature and the earth, which in turn will also bring about a transformation in relationships among human beings. To achieve these inter-related goals, it is not enough simply to rely on technical and managerial solutions or on some cosmetic changes in the model of development being followed. Change of paradigm calls for a new vision, attitude, and values, which religions, despite their tainted history, can still provide, especially by developing appropriate eco-theologies. For, as John Clammer notes in his contribution in this issue of *Concilium*, theology is still one discipline that attempts to maintain an integral vision of reality.

The direction and inspiration we expect from an inter-religious eco-theology is one that will help humanity to realize the primordial bonds that bind together everything that exists. It could be described metaphorically as Indra's net with jewel knots connecting the whole of reality, and each jewel reflecting all other jewels in an infinite process. From the realization of interconnectedness and interdependence flows the attitude of empathetic compassion toward all creatures and a deep sense of solidarity among human beings. We should expect an eco-theology to help us realize also the fluid and provisional sense of the borders separating various realms of reality – the human, the cosmic, and the divine.

The development of inter-religious eco-theology would presuppose that each religious tradition critically examine its own belief-system, world-views, and values to see to what extent they have been responsible for the ecological crisis, particularly by promoting a short-sighted anthropocentrism. On the other hand, the same religious traditions could today provide us with elements for overcoming the crisis and entering into a harmonious relationship with nature and the whole of reality.

Inter-religious eco-theology needs to challenge an insulated understanding of the individual placed above the community and nature and help stem the tide of competition and accumulation of wealth – so heavily responsible for bringing about the present ecological crisis. Eco-theology has also to face the challenge of bringing about radical changes in the present-day structures of economy and development, which means that it has to become truly political in its praxis.

Notes

1. As quoted in Roger S. Gottlieb (ed.), *The Oxford Handbook of Religion and Ecology*, Oxford: Oxford University Press, 2006, p. 12.
2. Nikos Kazantzakis, *Report to El Greco*, New York: Simon and Schuster, 1965.
3. Cf. Raimundo Panikkar, *The Vedic Experience. An Anthology of the Vedas for Modern Man and Contemporary Celebration*, Pondicherry: All India Books, 1977. For the earth see *Atharva Veda* XII.1:

Untrammelled in the midst of men, the Earth
Adored with heights and gentle slopes and plains
Bears plants and herbs of various healing powers
May she spread wide for us, afford us joy.

Bearer of all things, hoard of treasures rare
Sustaining mother, Earth the golden-breasted
Who bears the Sacred Universal Fire,
Whose spouse is Indra – may she grant us wealth. (p. 123)

4. Christopher Key Chapple and Mary Evelyn Tucker (eds), *Hinduism and Ecology*, Harvard: Harvard University Press, 2000, p. 152.

5. Cf. Karl Rahner, 'Christology within an Evolutionary View', in *Theological Investigations*, vol. 5, London: Darton, Longman & Todd, 1966; Piet Schoonenberg, 'Evolution – Hominisation – Geschichte', in *Auf Gott hin denken*, Freiburg: Herder, 1986, pp. 129 ff.

6. There is an effort today to absorb the Hindu heritage without acknowledging its contribution, as when some Western authors speak of *panentheism*. See the various contributions in Philip Clayton and Arthur Peacoke (eds), *In Whom We Live and Move and Have Our Being. Panentheistic Reflections on God's Presence in a Scientific World*, Grand Rapids, MI: Eerdmans, 2004.

7. The Dalai Lama in his preface to Julia Martin (ed.), *Ecological Responsibility. A Dialogue with Buddhism*, Delhi: Tibetan House and Sri Satguru Publication, 1997, p.vii.

8. Cf. Gottlieb, *The Oxford Handbook of Ecology and Religion, op.cit.* pp. 96–7.

9. *Ibid.* p. 97.

10. Cf. Vandana Shiva, *Staying Alive. Women, Ecology and Survival in India*, London: Zed Books, 1989.

11. Rahner, *op.cit.*, p. 160.

12. Cf. Lynn White, Jr., 'The Historical Roots of Our Ecological Crisis', in *Science* 155 (10 Mar. 1967), pp. 1203–7. This article generated a lot of world-wide debate.

13. Dionysius the Areopagite, *On Divine Names*, 1:6. See *Pseudo-Dionysius. The Complete Works*, Mahwah, NJ: Paulist Press, 1987, p. 56. (I have made some adaptations to the translation, especially in the use of inclusive language.)

14. Vinay Lal, 'Too Deep for Deep Ecology: Gandhi and the Ecological Vision of Life', in Chapple and Tucker, *Hinduism and Ecology, op. cit.*, p. 206.

15. Cf. Erich Neumann, *The Great Mother*, New York: Pantheon Books, 1955.

16. Cf. John A. Grim, *Indigenous Traditions and Ecology*, Harvard: Harvard University Press, 2001.

Eco-theology: Epistemological Approaches

ALICIO CÁCERES AGUIRRE

In order to establish an inter-disciplinary dialogue between ecology and theology, with a view to contributing to interpretation of the environmental crisis in its deeper aspects and, on this basis, suggesting routes to personal, community, and global transformation, it is pertinent to examine the field of preconceptions, notions, and imaginaries that underlie the question at hand. In other words, putting forward a theology of ecology requires us to clarify our understanding of both ecology and theology and to identify areas where they impinge on one another. We need to be precise about what is 'ecological' in theology and what is 'theological' in ecology.

To start with, there is clearly a semantic problem. The words 'ecology' and 'theology' have a variety of meanings. For example, today we have an abundance of terms such as ecosystem, eco-technology, eco-tourism, ecologism, eco-feminism and the like, or we readily speak of the ecological crisis, ecological consciousness, our ecological footprint, ecological politics, and so on without, as a general rule, reflecting rigorously on what these terms actually mean.

I. From etymology to epistemology

The prefix 'eco' derives (as does 'ecu') from the Greek *oikos*, meaning house, home, hearth, and all that these terms imply. Several contemporary linguistic studies confirm that the *oikos* is not merely the physical structure of the dwelling but the relationships produced within a house, which constitute the identity of a family. *Logos* for its part refers to study of, treatise on, or discussion about something and implies the systematic use of reason to form words that describe a particular reality.

The first use of the word 'ecology' is attributed to the German biologist Ernst Haeckel (1834–1919), who combined *oikos* and *logos* to refer to 'the sum totals of knowledge concerning the economy of nature, the investigation of all relationships of animals to both their inorganic and organic

55

surroundings, including above all their friendly and hostile interactions with those animals and plants to which they are directly or indirectly related. In a word, ecology is the study of all the complex inter-relationships that Darwin referred to as the conditions of the struggle for existence'.[1]

From this first definition to the present, variations on the 'ecology' concept have appeared, owing to three factors:

(1) Acceptance and situation of human beings as part of the network of relationships of living organisms, inasmuch as they interact in either a 'hostile' or a 'friendly' fashion with their living surroundings. This necessarily led to a dialogue between natural sciences and social sciences.

(2) The rise of new concepts such as 'environment' and 'ecosystem'. The first is related to the concept of *Umwelt* (Spanish *ambiente*, French *ambience*, etc. – *trans.*) first propounded in 1919 by Jacob von Uexküll (1864–1944), meaning the manner in which living beings perceive their surroundings, which determines their behaviour and so their survival. The second, generally held to have been coined by Sir Arthur Tansley (1871–1955) in 1935 (or by Roy Clapham in 1930), is a contraction of the words 'ecological system' and is used to describe the complexity not only of organisms but also of the physical factors that form the environment. The word 'system' is derived from the Greek *Synistanai*, meaning 'to unite or combine'. The formal description of the system concept is the work of the biologist Ludwig Von Bertalanffy (1901–72),[2] on 'A General Systems Theory'. He took understanding of systems beyond the physical systems studied by mathematicians by extending his research to organisms as entities that are inseparable from their environment and therefore cannot be studied in isolation. This generated a different logic of the understanding of life: an eco-logy.

(3) The dimension of scale of the *oikos* insofar as it is no longer just the living space of one species but the planetary and cosmic character of life. In this way, ecology went from being concern with relationships affecting animals and ourselves to a way of approaching the inter-relationships of all living beings in this house we call Planet Earth.

II. The roots of the ecological crisis

Since the publication of the Club of Rome report on 'The Limits of Growth' and the U.N convocation of a first summit on 'The Human Environment', held in Stockholm in 1972, polemic on the population explosion and the environmental impact of the human race has grown continually, turning 'ecology' into a term in daily use, though it still has a multiplicity of inter-pretations and meanings.

There have been many attempts at classifying these currents. Felix Gattari has posed three understandings of ecology: (1) natural, referring to inter-actions with the environment; (2) social, referring to relationships within society; and (3) mental, referring to personal subjectivity.[3] Leonardo Boff, for his part, has added another, which he calls 'integral ecology': this includes the first three but views them from a religious viewpoint, in the sense of re-linking them to the Mystery, the divinity, the source of life.[4] Roy H. May has extended the models in the hermeneutical discussion to six: (1) conventional ecology, based on technological and economic criteria that consider nature in its instrumental value, as a resource, a source of capital; (2) 'majordomic' ecology, derived from the biblical outlook in which there is a God who del-egates the administration of the *oikos* to human beings; (3) social ecology, which integrates social, economic, and political questions into the crisis of our bio-physical surroundings out of concern for justice; (4) deep ecology, which challenges the values of modernity and opts for a 'bio-centrism': that is, an egalitarianism in valuing all forms of life; (5 and 6) the integration of ecological concerns into the feminist movement and liberation theology have given rise to eco-feminism and Latin American eco-theology, respectively.[5]

Such a diversity of understandings of ecology reflects the innumerable explanations of the crisis that is affecting the blue, watery, globe of Earth. As we delve ever deeper into its causes, so further dimensions and features of this 'new' ecology emerge. So the technical and economic explanation pro-duces an ecology that places the stress on technological solutions. A social ecology is more concerned with critique of social structures and types of civilization. A deep ecology takes up the theme of values, giving space to ethical, moral, spiritual, and religious approaches. There is a generally dis-cernible shift from might be called an 'outer' to an 'inner' ecology.

III. Ecology: from science to paradigm

From the scientific point of view, ecology helps us to understand nature and to interpret reality, answering the question of what is happening and explain-ing why what happens does happen. Specialists in ecology provide a great service to humanity by trying to explain the structure, dynamics, and func-tioning of ecosystems. Other persons and groups then use these scientific data to build new understandings that can make the continuance of life on the planet possible. These then become fuel for ecological movements (more concerned with the conservation and preservation of nature) and environmental movements (closer to the debate on developmental models and their economic, political, and cultural components).

Speaking of ecology as a great paradigm, or of the ecological paradigm, is something different: this refers to a whole set of philosophical presuppositions putting forward a vision and manner of understanding and interpreting reality. Edgar Morin's suggestion of the need to 'ecologize' our thinking and Gregory Bateson's contribution on the subject of cultivating an 'ecology of mind' belong in this context.[6] The Third World Forum on Theology and Liberation, 'Water, Land, Theology for Another Possible World', held in Belém, in Brazil, at the beginning of 2009, tended to opt for integral ecology and to consider it not so much as a science on its own but more as a great paradigm for understanding the dynamics and relationships of life.

Ecology, then, is not confined to study of relationships with that other, the non-human, that makes up our bio-physical surroundings and is usually called nature, but involves cultural dynamics (social, economic, political, religious), their underlying world-views, the reasoning that underpins them, and, in general, the sum total of mental images that describe relationships with oneself, with others, with 'the other', and with God (or whatever image one has of transcendence and giving meaning to life).

The emerging ecological paradigm recognizes that nature is a subject, a 'someone' (Mother Earth, Sister Earth, Gaia, and so on), and that we human beings form a part of her. Furthermore, the believing approach is moving beyond the idea of conceiving of what exists as a 'natural resource' and making space for its intrinsic value as creation and therefore related to the Creator God. This is the context in which voices are heard calling the ecological crisis something rooted in the Judeo-Christian tradition (Lynn White), a moral concern (Pope John Paul II), the result of a loss of '*re-ligio*' (Leonardo Boff), the product of a crisis of perception and therefore of Spirituality (Fritjof Capra).[7] The identity of eco-theology comes to be seen as a feeling-thinking-acting on the relationship of God with God's creation: a *logos* on the *theos* inter-relating with the *oikos*.

IV. Environmental philosophy and eco-theology

This trilogy of concepts refers us back to the relations between God and the House and is concerned with living together in the latter. However, it would be a massive pretension to attempt a discourse on God, since 'God is not the monopoly of any human tradition: not of those called "theist" or of those badly named believing. Nor is God the "object" of any thought. Any discourse that sought to imprison God in any ideology would be sectarian.'[8] Reference to God is in metaphorical terms, since, rather than being a concept, the word 'god' is a symbol mediated by culture, and it always indicates a specific life-experience. This is why we have to recognize that the Mystery is evoked from mental images, models, or imaginaries of God, and this means that all visions of God are partial.

So bringing the question of God into ecology, in order to do eco-theology, involves reference to the meaning of life and understanding of the cosmos. This is why we have to take account of questions from environmental philosophy if we are to prevent the reality we call god becoming detached from human or earthly reality. The two main questions are: (1) Are human beings part of nature? and (2) Is nature an object or a subject? Whatever the answer, this will have implications for constructing theological thinking on the subject.

Human beings 'are' nature: they do not stand outside it. Genetics prove that we are part of the evolutionary chain and related to all forms of life. Nevertheless, it is worth pointing out that there is a difference between feeling ourselves to be part of Gaia (when there is an intimate link to nature) and calling her 'Mother Earth' (filial relationship) or 'Sister Earth' (sibling relationship). The characteristics of these relationships cannot be taken for granted, since they define a type of environmental ethic and are at the root of how we understand eco-theology.

Of course, from this point of view, if we reject the expression 'natural resources', it can no longer be seen as valid to speak of 'human resource'. During the 2009 Forum there was a noticeable tendency to place the intrinsic value of nature above its instrumental value – evidence of a strong movement of reaction against utilitarianism in relationships among human beings and between ourselves and nature. Furthermore, faith that is born as response to God's self-revelation, self-communication, indicates that nature 'is' God's creation. This makes the category of 'creation' supremely important for the work of eco-theology. Understanding nature as creation in fact makes a substantial difference. We can no longer see nature as 'there' and ourselves as 'here', since we are all creation.

Stating that all that exists is creation leads to the image of a Creator God. But what sort of Creator? Within the Judeo-Christian tradition, Antony Campbell, SJ, has identified three models:[9] (1) unguided creation: God is an irresponsible being who creates the world and leaves it to run its course; (2) guided creation: God is like a sort of puppet-master who decides the

course of the universe down to its smallest details; (3) risk-taking creation:
God goes on creating 'from within' and 'from below', becoming sharer and
participant in the future of the world.

But where is this Creator? Transcendent, outside history? Or immanent,
within matter? Or, as Boff asks, transparent and so immanent-transcendent?
If this is the case, then creation is a divine sacrament – the *shekinah*, the
divine dwelling.[10] At the 2009 Forum, the tendency was to recognize God
as being in creation, living in water, air, earth, fire. . . . All this leads to discussion on pantheism (God is everything) and panentheism (God in everything). Epistemological understanding of the type of relationship between
God and creation brings consequences for the way we do eco-theology and
the existential questions that follow from it.

Furthermore, understanding creation as *oikos* has its limits. Eco-feminism
has produced one critique of the house metaphor for its patriarchal, outward-
looking, and utilitarian implications. Sallie McFague has proposed the metaphor of creation as the body of God.[11] We all form part of the divine body
and this lies at the root of the sacred nature of caring for it. At the Forum,
some participants insisted on this bodily dimension of creation for the way
it opened up new spheres of discernment and debate. Perhaps the term 'ecology' is no longer adequate to indicate the action that is required. If this
were so, 'eco-theology' would be based on a mistaken approach. It is not so
much the object under investigation or the question that would change: what
would change are the epistemological mediations for interpreting life, for
understanding and explaining what us happening, why what happens does
happen, and what God has to do with what happens.

V. Ecology and images of God

All this makes it worth thinking through (which is already eco-theologizing!)
the implications of adopting the idea that, rather than dwelling in the body of
God, we form part of the body of God. In this context, we need to explore,
for example, Luiz Carlos Susin's image of a living house, or to think of ourselves in our mother's womb.[12] Following this line, the various images of God
as champion, spokesperson, companion, friend, father, mother, need to be
complemented by the metaphor of God the Ecosystem, as a product of the
contribution of ecology to theology (theo-ecology, rather than eco-theology).
This is a God understood as an ecosystem of love, as an infinite network of
loving relationships. In this way, we can join Andrés Torres Queiruga in stating that God is no longer so much Love (noun) as Loving (verb), that God

'is' movement, dynamism, inter-relationship.[13] God 'is' loving, and whilst he loves, he saves, 're-creates'; that is, God 'is' perpetual creation. God 'is being' to the extent that there are relationships of love, generating a sort of vital atmosphere that envelops us. Could this be what Paul was referring to when he stood in front of the Areopagus and stated, 'In him we live and move and have our being' (Acts 17.28–9)?

This implies a transformation of our idea of God. There is a difference between understanding God as 'another' (person, father, mother, friend) and understanding God as an environment, a means, a web, something like the water that permeates the whole of life in a pond. In this case, eco-theology has to concern itself not just with the structural problems of this house we call Earth but with the ties of love within it. Where love is, there is God. God exists wherever there is love. Love is always a relationship. Eco-theology has to be concerned with the ecology of love.

The many variables in the epistemological presuppositions referring to 'God', 'human beings', and 'creation' clearly provide sufficient reason for there not being one single eco-theology. We have, rather, to speak of eco-theologies. So Rosemary Radford Ruether distinguished three currents: (1) the propositions of Matthew Fox, based on a spirituality of creation; (2) the believing evolutionism of Pierre Teilhard de Chardin; (3) the process theology of Alfred Whitehead.[14] For his part, K. C. Abraham has summed up Christian approaches to creation as: (1) ascetic-monastic; (2) sacramental-eucharistic; (3) liberative and in solidarity with.[15]

Faced with this spread of approaches, Raimundo Panikkar has posed cosmo-theandric intuition as a critique of the Western separation of the God-world-human being trilogy and proposed an integrating view of life.[16] In this view, the paradigm of eco-theological construction would change radically, coming to see God as being essentially and actually in nature, and nature as including human beings. Given the complex character of existence as brought out by ecology, this way of looking at things requires us to move beyond the logic of linear thinking and to adopt a holistic approach, seeking an overall vision of the whole with its parts and the parts with the whole, making use of general system and process theory as well as exercising inter- and trans-disciplinarity.

This involves the need for recourse to the explanations put forward by the empirical-analytical sciences and establishing a dialogue between them and the hermeneutical and emancipatory sciences. Theology will thereby take on its task of quest for meaning, in attentive listening to the God-Love in self-communication in creation. In this way, eco-theology will find its place, as

Bernard Lonergan says,[17] as mediation between the cultural matrix indicated by the present ecological crisis and the proposition of life that stems from the gospel and from all those life-experiences that lead to the wisdom of cosmic communion.

Such an eco-theology does not belong to any one religion in particular. The global nature of the crisis invites us all to reflect in terms of religious pluralism. This means adopting a 'macro-ecumenical' viewpoint, remembering that the word *oikumene*, ecumenism, meaning unity in the inhabited world, derives from the root *oikos*, which also produces the terms 'ecology' and 'economy'. This is quite different from each religion turning back to a quest for its own 'eco-sources', producing specific outcomes such as Christian eco-theology, Islamic eco-theology, or Jewish eco-theology, to name only the monotheistic traditions. The horizon of eco-theology is the reflection of the God-nature-human being triad in search of immanent-transcendent meaning.

Even so, we need to recognize, in all humility, the limitations of understanding in faith, since in order to speak of God we need to speak with God, to be in communion with, in dialogue with, in search of, and open to Love. In this sense, theology is a second act, following a silence, as both Gustavo Gutiérrez and Panikkar have stated.[18]

Spirituality is the basis of theology; without spirituality there is no theology. But at the same time a theology without transforming action is sterile and ineffective.

In the eco-theological approach, beauty, sorrow, emptiness, love, and liberation are some of the dynamisms that make contact with the Mystery possible. The dramatic destruction of ecosystems, the agony of the poor who have no water or land or sanitation to enable them live with dignity, the concentration of goods in the hands of a few, the threat to life from nuclear weapons, chemical products, and biological manipulations, coupled with uncertainty in the face of the environmental implications of cloning and genetic modification, all form fresh contrasts to the colours of toucans and macaws, the splendour of waterfalls, the sacred white of snows, the sound of wind on the mountains, the blessings of corn and wheat, the fascination of the atom, the charms of the double helix, of the awe produced by constellations and galaxies. Ultimately, every relationship leads to God, every relationship leads to love, to the final meaning of existence, experience of the Mystery.

If theological thinking is the second act – and liberation theology sees praxis as the starting-point – then liberating action has an essential spiritual component. This means seeing spirituality not as one more reasoned theological treatise deriving from morals, or even as a separate part of life: it is the Spirit flowing like sap from the roots of theology. Therefore we have to move from eco-theology to the interpretation offered by eco-wisdom.

VI. From eco-theologies to eco-wisdom

The term 'eco-wisdom' brings several currents together. Felix Gattari saw it as the outcome of the three ecologies (environmental, social, and mental); Raimundo Panikkar and Arne Naess have independently developed the term, the first more in the direction of mystical theology, the second in the philosophical terms of deep ecology. This convergence provides guidelines for as new approach to reality.

There is still a need to assign a fresh meaning to the term, however. 'Eco-wisdom', the wisdom of the *oikos*, has to be understood in two senses: (1) learning the wisdom of creation, its laws for being able to live in harmony. This is not a matter of 'taming' nature, but of a new alliance based on understanding, respect, and admiration; (2) learning the wisdom of living together within the *oikos*, with a greater consciousness that the Earth is the common home of living beings and their life-support systems. So the shift from eco-theology to eco-wisdom is based on two aspects: (1) the insufficiency of *logos* for taking account of love and the need to integrate symbolic reason with analytical and instrumental reason; (2) openness to other forms of reason that have either been in existence for centuries or are being generated in emergent groups, representing wisdom that is not always organized and that cannot be enclosed within the parameters of Western logic.

At the 2009 World Forum, there was a noticeable sort of tension between eco-theology and eco-wisdom. On the one hand, there was the effort to construct an eco-theology in the moulds of theology based on the praxis of liberation, which would follow the option for the poor while incorporating the environmental question and would organize its concepts and methods to enter into dialogue with biblical narratives and the message of the Kingdom. On the other was acceptance of the eco-wisdom of indigenous and Afro peoples, the wisdom that springs from exiled, expropriated, and impoverished communities and from those with only precarious access to drinking water and basic sanitation. This wisdom tends to remain on the level of oral tradition and to express itself in story and symbol. It is not a wisdom that lets itself be ensnared in ratiocination or encoded in systematic treatises.

The terms ecology, eco-theology, and eco-wisdom are of course not mutually exclusive. In the case of Christianity, understanding Christ as the Wisdom of God even facilitates dialogue with other forms of wisdom and helps to tighten bonds of love with the rest of creation as a framework for living in mutual respect and communion in diversity. This means that the epistemological turn that integrates affectivity and reason implies a sacramental view of the world. It is not enough to understand the world (with our minds); we also have to comprehend it (with our hearts). It is vital that we recover the affective dimension, the right to tenderness, in order to bring human life and ecosystems into balance. A mysticism based on austerity and non-violence, solidarity and service, care and compassion, can become the pillar to which all are drawn and on which we can build platforms for an authentic ecological ethic, which can bring about the sustainability of life, to the greater Glory of God, which is none other than human beings living fully in harmony with creation.

Translated by Paul Burns

Notes

1. E. Haeckel, *General Morphology of Organisms; General Outlines of the Science of Organic Forms based on Mechanical Principles through the Theory of Descent as reformed by Charles Darwin*, Berlin, 1866.
2. First described in 'An Outline of General System Theory', in *British Journal for the Philosophy of Science*, 1 (1950), 139–64; see also his *General System Theory: Foundation, Development, Application*, revised ed., New York: George Braziller, 1968.
3. F. Gattari, *As três ecologias*, Campinas: Papirus, 1988.
4. L. Boff, *Ecologia: grito da terra, grito dos pobres*, Petrópolis: Vozes, 1995 (Eng, trans. by P. Berryman, *Cry of the Earth, Cry of the Poor*, Maryknoll, NY: Orbis, 1995). See also *Ecology, Cry of the Earth, Cry of the Poor, Concilium* 1995/5, ed. L. Boff and V. Elizondo.
5. R. H. May, *Ética y medio ambiente: Hacia una vida sostenible*, San José; DEI, 2002,
6. E. Morin, *Les sept savoirs necessaries à l'éducation du futur* (Eng. trans. *Seven Complex Lessons in Education for the Future*), Paris: UNESCO, 1999; G. Bateson, *Steps to an Ecology of Mind*, London: Paladin, 1973.
7. See L. White, 'The Historical Roots of Our Ecological Crisis', *Science* 155 (1967) 1203–7 (reprinted in D. Van De Veer and C. Pierce, eds., *Environmental Ethics and Policy Book*, Belmont, CA: Wadsworth, 1994), pp. 45–51; John Paul II, 'Message for World Day of Peace, 1 January 1990', Vatican City, 8 Dec. 1989; L. Boff, *Ecologia, op.cit.*; F. Capra, *The Web of Life: A New Scientific Understanding of Living Systems*, New York: Anchor, 1996.

8. R. Panikkar, *The Experience of God: Icons of the Mystery*, Minneapolis: Augsburg Fortress, 2006 (here Sp. trans., p. 12).

9. A. F. Campbell, 'Evolutionary Theory and Biblical Discourse', in *Concilium* 2000/1, pp. 92–101.

10. J. Moltmann, 'Sobre la teología ecológica', *Páginas* 141 (June 1996).

11. S. McFague, *Models of God: Theology for an Ecological, Nuclear Age*, Philadelphia: Fortress Press, 1987; *idem. The Body of God: An Ecological Theology,*: Minneapolis: Fortress Press, 1993.

12. L. C. Susin, 'Mãe Terra que nos sustenta e governa: por uma teologia de sustentabilidade', in Sociedade de Teologia e Ciências da Religião (ed.), *Sustentabilidade da vida e espiritualidade*, São Paulo; Paulinas, 2008, pp. 191–214.

13. A. Torres Queiruga, 'A imaxe de Deus na nova situación cultural', *Encrucillada* 27 (2003), 221–43; also in *Selecciones de Teología* 170 (2004), 103–16; see also *idem.* '¿Dónde está Dios? La pregunta en el mundo actual', at http://www.iglesiaviva.org/223/223-12-TORRES.pdf. p.42; 'Creer de otra manera', at http://sevicioskoinonia.org/biblioteca/bibliodatos1.html?QUEIRUGA, p. 12.

14. R. Radford Ruether, *Gaia and God: An Ecofeminist Theology of Earth Healing*, San Francisco: HarperSanFrancisco, 1993.

15. K. C. Abraham, 'A Theological Response to the Ecological Crisis', in D. G. Hallman (ed.), *Ecotheology: Voices from South and North*, Maryknoll, NY: Orbis, 1994.

16. R. Panikkar, *Ecosofia. Para una espiritualidad de la tierra*, Madrid: San Pablo, 1994.

17. B. Lonergan, *Method in Theology*, New York: Herder & Herder, 1972.

18. G. Gutiérrez, 'Lenguaje teológico: plenitud del silencio', *Páginas* 137 (Feb. 1996), 82; Panikkar, *op.cit.*, 7.

3. The Challenge of Praxis

Environmental Theologies as Processes of Ecclesiogenesis and Common Discernment

JACQUES HAERS

I. Lessons of European history

Environmental challenges, of which today climate change and energy consumption are major features, are 'glocal' (global/local) realities. Although we experience their impact in our immediate context, they concern the whole planet. Therefore, it is shortsighted to restrict ourselves merely to our local reality without taking into account a global perspective. Nevertheless, the views we have on these challenges are locally contextual: Brazilians, Indonesians, Australians, Somalis, Indians, Canadians, and Europeans perceive matters differently. I am a West European Roman Catholic theologian, a member of one of the wealthiest regions of the planet enjoying an unsustainably heavy ecological foot. I am aware that I should tread carefully in these matters, but I also know that European history over its past century teaches some costly and precious lessons, which may prove of good service to theologians who address today's global environmental challenges. From this perspective I offer a contribution while hoping that fellow theologians from other regions of the globe will correct me for my blind spots. I highlight four of what I consider to be important lessons of European history.

First, Europeans know about the ambiguities of being caught up in structures and patterns of violence that they themselves have caused and continue to maintain. This is true for much of the violence during Europe's past 100 years: two world wars more horrifying than anything people could have imagined, murderous political regimes that set out as ideals for a better life amidst societal chaos, social injustice veiled as necessary for economic development, colonial exploitation clouded as the spreading of civilization,

and the neo-colonial attitudes of fortress Europe in a globalized world, testi-
fy to complex and entrapping structures of violence. Not surprisingly, issues
of guilt and accountability regularly surface in Europe while, at the same
time, people feel discouraged and powerless when confronting structures
of violence that seem out of control. Of course, often, individual human
beings can and should be held accountable to various degrees, but the situation is more complex and tragic. People may feel overwhelmed by structures
of violence that escape their control, disempower them, dominate them,
and ensnare them. In the insightful *After Ten Years*, an introduction to his
letters from prison, Dietrich Bonhoeffer describes the need for discernment
amidst human powerlessness against perverse evil structures that present
themselves as desirable and morally good. Of course, these tragic ambiguities
should never allow the voices of those who suffer violence to be smothered.

Second, Europeans attempt today to solve their conflicts by engaging in
common projects that bind them together into the reality of a new common
life. To move from violent war toward sustainable peace, Europeans learned
to collaborate by recognizing diversity in cultures and languages as an asset
and not as a threat. At the heart of the European process of unification lies
community building as a way of conflict resolution. Europe has learned this
lesson within its own borders; it is not clear whether it will be capable and
willing to move in the same way within the global world, engaging in a common worldwide project. Here lies an opportunity to engage in a response to
global environmental challenges.

Third, Europe has a history of colonial violence with the non-European
world, assuming its own civilization and cultures to be superior to those of
the rest of the world and sometimes using Christianity to make the point.
The processes of colonization and decolonization have left the former
colonies and European colonizing countries with a bitter aftertaste and
a deep need for reconciliation that should not, however, become a clever
cover-up for neo-colonial attitudes in a global world. These realities and
feelings have to be taken into account when Western European theologians provide their opinion on global matters and ecological issues. There
will always be the understandable suspicion that Europe is playing power
games to protect its own wealth and interests by preaching an environmental gospel to others.

Fourth, a common Europe would not be possible without the visions of
great visionaries such as Jean Monnet, Robert Schuman, and Jacques Delors.
Visionary leadership, in this case to avoid further wars in Europe, brings hope
and perspective, without offering well defined blueprints. Rather, it awakes

enthusiasm and energy, and indicates a direction the endpoint of which is not yet clear, but which nevertheless acts as an attractor to shape current attitudes and actions that embody and, at the same time, clarify the vision. Such a vision for Europe aims at interdependent life together. Europeans embody this through creating economic and political interdependence.

These four lessons – the ambiguities of structures of violence, collaboration in processes of community building through common projects, the overcoming of colonial power games, and the need for vision – suggest theological perspectives that may be helpful when thinking about global environmental challenges. They are complex signs of the time that are human-made but escape our control, while also revealing God's call. Such a call lies in processes of community building that we could address as ecclesiogenesis and common discernment; as efforts at reconciling creatively the differences in our world and at tackling critically our power games; and as symbolic and liturgical expressions of a vision of hope that can be enshrined theologically in our understanding of creation and of the Kingdom of God. It is these which the remainder of this article will address.

II. Four key experiences

(a) Today's environmental challenges are complex 'signs of the time': they touch important life and death issues not only for human beings but also for the planet as a whole, and they constitute a key *locus theologicus*, where an empowering and life-giving encounter with God is revealed. Similarly to how Europeans are prisoners of violence they both cause and suffer as it becomes a structure that overwhelms them destructively, while they nevertheless continue to maintain it, today all of us are caught up in a worldwide environmental crisis that human actions have brought about and continue to deepen. Indeed, there can be no doubt about the anthropogenic causes of global warming or about how our competitive and insatiable hunger for energy and natural resources constitutes unsustainable greed. Consumerist so-called Western lifestyles are unsustainable in the long run, most certainly on a planetary scale. Moreover, it is unacceptably unjust that these lifestyles are limited to some at the expense of others. Nature, our environment, has been so taxed that it is looking for new global balances, a process that we do not control. In a cruel paradox, the poorest amongst us, who are least capable of organizing themselves to face the consequences of environmental changes, will suffer the most in a crisis that has been caused by the lifestyles of the richest amongst us.

The changes that are now taking place in nature are complex, multifaceted, dangerous, beyond our common understanding, and running out of control. They have huge social impact and will physically alter the face of the earth. Our classical mix for solving such problems, using a combination of scientific and technological recipes, complemented by economical, political and military measures, will not do the trick this time. We need to move toward a new way of life, and that requires also spiritual attitudes as embodied, for example, in the religious vows. To deepen their reflections on sin, suffering and hope – taking into account a new balance of responsibility and accountability in the midst of structures of evil – theologians will have to rely on serious trans-disciplinary research, for example combining IPCC work, the thought of a sociologist such as Zygmunt Bauman, and theological and spiritual perspectives.

We also now know that dramatic environmental changes are already taking place. Serious global crisis management has become inevitable. Theologically speaking, our incarnation into the world, embracing the reality of the planet by creating sustainable life together amongst human beings and with nature, requires concrete and common decisions about how to face disasters and threats to the lives of millions of people as well as to many other creatures. Churches and religions are well equipped to play an active role of global solidarity. Indeed, they constitute worldwide networks and can rely on the resources of people in the field, of institutes of learning, of media of communication, of spirituality, liturgies, and sacraments, and of political influence. Not preparing at this very practical level of incarnation constitutes at this moment a grave sin of omission. Building a worldwide community of solidarity means reflecting (*re-legere*) on how to deeply connect reality (*re-ligare*) in structures and patterns of solidarity and compassion, in the face of great suffering. This is a challenge for religion today.

The environmental crisis is so threatening and complex that many people are caught up in a process of denial. Their eco-scepticism can take on many forms: not paying attention, fundamentalist perspectives such as staunch creationism that resists any scientific approach that would make one face reality, denial of the anthropogenic features of the crisis, claiming that the changes of lifestyle that are required will increase worldwide poverty and injustice. Religions and the Churches have a profound responsibility in addressing the despair and the fears that generate eco-scepticism, so as to allow for a sound sense of reality required to address the challenge. Gaining insight by trusting the results of serious science, and confronting oneself with the suffering of those who as the poorest amongst us pay the highest price in environmental change, may help us all to consider the ways to redesign the structure of our lives together in a sustainable way.

(b) The core challenge in the environmental crisis is to engage in the common project of a sustainable world, through which we grow into a more connected community amongst human beings worldwide and with nature. The goal is sustainable life together, in which all beings are treated in a way that respects their being 'creatures', i.e. loved and respected by God and, therefore, deserving the respect due to God. The building of sustainable life together and the respect of creational dignity in life and death, require common discernment in which the voices of all are heeded, particularly those voices that are in danger of being forgotten and not counted, be they the voices of excluded human beings or of other creatures, or even of creation as a whole.

The Christian experience concerns encounters and life together. It is profoundly relational at various levels: relations with God, with oneself, with other human beings, with nature and creation. Christians sometimes forget that the good message (*eu-angellion*) of Jesus aims at our capacity to live together, even with those people whom we exclude from this togetherness, and even in processes of forgiveness and reconciliation that reach out beyond our abilities. Many words in the Christian tradition express this relational reality: creation, the Kingdom of God, the Church, Trinity, etc. I will unfold their visionary power further on, and concentrate now on the meaning of the words creation and church.

The word 'creation' has many dimensions that are crucial to a theology of the environment and that have also sometimes been neglected, mainly because we tend to focus on creation merely as the beginning of time or as the relation of God to the individual human being. Creation refers to the whole of creation, to the world, the universe as a dynamic whole of interconnected relationships. A part of creation – the human being is such a part – cannot be cut off from creation as if it were independent from creation. Moreover, creation is not merely the sum of the creatures that are found in it – the question as to what precisely should be considered a creature is already difficult to answer with precision – but is also constituted by the relationships between all its parts, and because these relationships constitute a web of creation, creation as a whole can be perceived as a living and dynamic creature itself. In this approach, human beings are parts of the larger creature 'earth', or of the creature 'creation itself. They constitute a part of creation that creation has allowed to develop in itself as a recombination of some of its elements so as to give itself a new potential. Human beings, indeed, allow creation to reach a stage of self-awareness. In that sense they have a special place in creation, but they cannot be cut off from creation. This position, which allows us to understand why human beings are special in a creation they cannot be cut off from, I call 'relational anthropocentrism'. In their relationships to the rest of creation to which they belong, human beings enjoy an important status, while remaining creatures, the product of an evolutionary process in which a whole is created from components and the relationship between those components is such that the whole is more than the mere sum of the components. Karl Rahner, in this context, spoke about 'self-transcendence' (*Selbst-Ueberbietung*), while today we prefer to use the word 'emergence' suggested by new recent developments in scientific thought.

The creative interplay of diversity that creation unfolds as an opportunity for its further development, also characterizes the processes in which Christians build up their communities – communities amongst Christians, but also communities shared with non-Christians. These processes can be called ecclesiogenesis, as in them emerges church, communities of people called together by God to overcome and transform the conflicts between the members of these communities through reshaping the relationships between them, sometimes in the radical ways of forgiveness and reconciliation. The perspective of ecclesiogenesis can also be broadened and used to clarify the processes through which new sustainable relationships are built with God, amongst human beings and with nature, so as to address the environmental challenges. Today's worldwide crisis highlights, in a painful way, that the environmental challenge is of all times, that creation will never cease to demand the common effort of discerning which environmental relationships are life-giving and respectful of creational dignity. This process of discerning reorientation of fundamental creational relationships addresses the core of the Christian experience in a world of change, of life and death. It also addresses the evils of exclusion and perverted relationships in which others are disrespectfully used to serve one's interests. The preferential option for the poor unmasks such abusive relationships or exclusions as unjust by allowing those who suffer these exclusions and abuses to claim creational dignity born out of the relationship with God. In so doing, they claim this dignity not only for themselves, but for the whole of creation.

The relational features of reality that surface in the concept of creation and that determine the efforts at church building, have a universal scope: the community-building at the core of environmental theology has a universal scope, always tastes for more, wants to include the whole of creation and not only parts of it, even if, in the historical processes of community-building only limited communities are realized. It is a temptation to remain with the limited communities in which one feels at home and not to confront oneself with diversity beyond the borders of such limited communities. Community-building, therefore, when not universally oriented, i.e. when not open to include those who are not yet included, may turn out to be an instrument of exclusion. When, in these pages, I refer to processes of building sustainable communities respectful of creational dignity, I assume universal openness and holistic orientation, including not only human beings, but the whole of creation.

(c) Some are afraid of diversity as, in the conversations that arise out of the diversity and that create the urge to compare and to value through comparison, one's vulnerabilities and weakness may surface and may be abused in competitive power games. Colonial relationships, in which diversity is eliminated or made subservient, are a real threat. Feminist theologians have addressed these colonial and patriarchal temptations in the relationships with oneself, with God, with other human beings (particularly in the gender relationships), and with nature. Not surprisingly, eco-feminism, at this present time, is the most important theological current dealing with environmental challenges. Indeed, the environmental crisis is to a large extent due to colonial relationships with nature that arise in human beings who are tempted to set themselves over against the rest of creation, suggesting that also the Creator stands over against creation in a colonial relationship. Counteracting colonial approaches requires re-thinking the complex tension between transcendence and immanence, in the relationship between Creator and creation, in the relationships between human beings, and in the relationships between human beings and nature. Very helpful theological and spiritual metaphors may be in this context: '*mestizaje*', as developed in Virgilio Elizondo's thought; 'friendship' as a process of incarnation and trinitarian encounter as presented in the mystical experience of Egied Van Broeckhoven and in the Spiritual Exercises of Ignatius Loyola; and 'frontierspaces' of 'encounter' in the tension with 'borderlines of separation'.

Amidst the current environmental challenges it is important also to point to what could be called 'epistemological colonialism', consisting in the conviction that the crisis can be answered by what we have called the traditional mix of scientific, technological, economical, political, and military approaches. The reduction to this box of solutions is part of the problem, as it still uses a paradigm of control in which the controlling subject is set over against the controlled object, while what is required in the challenges that we study here is thought outside of the box: the issue is not control, but a different type of sustainable and respectful relations, that require humility and a change of attitudes. Here spirituality and theology, here the religions, may add their contribution, as well as philosophies – metaphysics and ontologies – based on the fundamental relational structures of reality.

(d) When one asks for the specificity of theology as a science, and for the specificity of its contribution in addressing the environmental challenges, one will have to point out its visionary and eschatological structure. In her thought on creation, Dorothee Sölle observed that one should be careful in calling our world a 'creation' as, in fact, it does not very much deserve that characterization. The word 'creation' seems to refer more to what we would want our world to be like, than to what our world in reality is. Nevertheless, Sölle continues to use the word 'creation' as, by revealing in the word 'creation' what this world can be and in its deepest depth is, we introduce a dynamic principle that allows us to change the world so as to unfold it as the creation it is. In the process of change we also discover, or begin to discover, what we mean when we use the word 'creation'.

Similarly, it seems easier to imagine hell than heaven. Hell can be easily illustrated from our daily realities of abuse, violence, war, torture, injustice, exclusion, poverty, etc. It is far more difficult to imagine what heaven or the Kingdom of God would look like, although in our experiences of love, of friendship, and of solidarity we intuit what the Kingdom may be. What does it mean to live together sustainably and in respect of creational dignity? This seems impossible in our concrete reality, and often people despair in their attempts to bring about such sustainable and respectful life together. Nonetheless, Christians answer the temptation to despair by referring to the vision of the Kingdom that arises in the relationship with God: although they cannot give a clear answer as to what the Kingdom looks like, God's commitment in Jesus of Nazareth provides them with a person to whom they can relate so as to commit their lives towards building the Kingdom in their concrete broken realities. In their praxis of attempting to build up sustainable and respectful communities for all and for the whole of creation, out of a discernment of their relationship with God in Jesus of Nazareth, they discover features of the Kingdom, which they will celebrate in their liturgies and sacraments, as if to put present that what cannot yet be present, as if to play the reality that concrete reality is not yet but will be. The eschatological tension consists in the tension between a vision that lies beyond our imagination and its broken concrete realization. To articulate this vision in concrete commitment requires communication and common discernment, a process in which community is constituted, which already embodies in the here and now, albeit in a broken way, the vision of the Kingdom. We touch again the twin concepts of common discernment and ecclesiogenesis.

In a world facing a daunting environmental crisis, which people are often tempted to present in apocalyptic terms, the need for vision is great, so as to resist the temptation to despair, and so as to discover, by entering into praxes of sustainable and dignified community building for all, the vision itself.

Conclusion

Four key experiences in Europe's recent history – the tragic dimensions of violence, the importance of community building, the temptation to colonial relationships, and the need for vision – have provided opportunities to highlight some key dimensions of a theology that attempts to address today's environmental challenges as an opportunity for theology in general to grow and deepen. Environmental theologies emphasize the profound relational features of the Christian experience at various levels: relations with God, with other human beings and with nature, and focus on sustainable community-building that is respectful of creational dignity and universally oriented. They explore processes of ecclesiogenesis, common discernment, emergence, and the eschatological tensions implied in the vision of the Kingdom of God. They address realities of human responsibilities and fears amidst complex environmental changes that escape human control and they attempt to understand the specific role of human beings as creatures amongst other creatures in creation. Environmental theologians are aware of their role in the trans-disciplinary processes necessary in the context of the global environmental crisis, as well as of their own responsibility to respond in a glocal way to the sufferings of human beings and nature caused by the environmental changes.

An Ascetic Theology, Spirituality, and Praxis

NEIL DARRAGH

Philosophies of growth that promote increasing standards of living still dominate much of the politics and expectations of governments in democratic countries. The motivations for adopting such philosophies include not just consumer gratification but also the promise of better access to health, education, housing, and security. The suspicion of this idea of economic growth has spread since it became apparent that the planet Earth is not an infinite entity, it is not an inexhaustible supply of energy and natural resources, and its ability to recycle human waste is limited. The hope that science could solve most of our problems has also become more modest and in any case expensive.

In contest with the philosophies of economic growth are the various forms of Earth spiritualities or green movements that promote ideas such as sustainability, thresholds of growth, 'better' rather than 'more', the precautionary principle, conservation rather than exploitation, and seek balance and integrity within the larger Earth processes. In this article I shall use the term 'Earth spirituality' as a general term to cover philosophies, theologies, spiritualities, or ideologies that promote such ideas.[1] The motivations for adopting such Earth spiritualities are less obvious than the motivations for seeking an increasing standard of living with its immediate benefits.

My intent in this article is to suggest that an important role for Christian theology is to respond to the continuing plea from many environmentalists for an articulation of the motivations, beyond the immediately practical, that would attract public support for sustainable environmental practices. Such a role would imply that theology (a) pay at least as much attention to the public as to the personal dimensions of Christian spirituality, and (b) draw on its own traditions of asceticism to deal with the restraints on desire that environmental sustainability requires.

I. Interweaving personal and public motivations

Some of the motivations for adopting Earth spiritualities are self-focused in that these spiritualities are seen as healthier or more spiritually wholesome or as paths to tranquillity in harmony with nature and the living Earth. While a consistent Earth spirituality involves an interior struggle with some of our most fundamental urges like greed, envy, and self-promotion, it is a struggle that is also carried on out there in the public forum. More responsible and less vandalistic human activity in the Earth depends upon the spread of such spiritualities into public policy. This implies a spirituality that is not just personal but is also a public engagement in society, an exercise in citizenship.[2] Its implications are social and structural, not just individual. It promotes the conditions for political change which can include economic incentives for environmental responsibility or legal sanctions on environmental polluters.

In this public forum, Earth spiritualities need a public justification in the sense that they need to provide reasons and arguments for their validity even to people who resist them politically or who dislike them personally. If they are to have public impact they need to provide reasons, motivations, or an attractive altruistic vision that is in contest with the attractions of personal gratification or the glamour of conspicuous consumption or the inertia of continuing business as usual. Earth spiritualities in the contemporary environment are spiritualities of constraint at least for the world's over-consumers, and to that extent are in contest with spiritualities of personal fulfilment, increasing choice, self-interest, and self-promotion. The reasons or motivations why *individuals* might adopt a spirituality or an ethic of environmental responsibility are many. The reasons or motivations that can make sense as *public policies* are much fewer.

There are already a number of reasons for adopting public policies of environmental sustainability that are acceptable and attractive in many societies. The most widespread is the argument from the accusation of future generations. What will your grand-children say to you when they see the polluted and depleted world your greed and self-indulgence has left them? Another argument effective in many countries is that of national identity. There are features of the natural environment which the citizens of that nation identify as an important part of their heritage and which are icons of their distinctive identity. A third more economic argument derives from benefits to trade and tourism. This argument becomes more potent as environmental concern becomes more widespread throughout the affluent world and consumer choices show preference for 'clean green' images attached to a product's origin or to a tourist destination.

An argument that has become prominent recently arises from widespread concerns over climate change and scarcities of oil, water, and soil. This is the 'new thrift' argument, which says essentially that we should cut back on energy use and carbon emissions because they are becoming too expensive, the clean-up will be even more expensive, as also will be scientific research into solutions; and they are going to be even more expensive if we don't reduce our consumption now. It is an argument for reduced consumption as a public responsibility not just as personal choice. It is mainly an economic argument, but it is not an argument for economic growth.

Flowing through and enriching these public motivations there still remain the more personal motivations such as a spiritual sensitivity toward and care for the wellbeing of other species or eco-systems and a sense of mystical participation in living Earth processes or of the presence of God in all beings.[1]

II. Information and its responses

Public information has been a major player in creating the conditions for the effectiveness of these motivations. Information about resource depletion and pollution has increased exponentially as scientific investigations have focused on the environment and as environmental indicators have become more sophisticated. Information is one of the powerful tools in this struggle. Information about the long-term effects of human action and the development of environmental indicators mean that we have more scientific knowledge than we ever had before. But responses to that information can still vary.

As the physical and biological sciences have increased our knowledge of the human impact on the planet, the social sciences have noted that knowing about environmental degradation and identifying the danger zones may produce different and not always desirable reactions. One such reaction is the 'eat, drink, and be merry' reaction governed simply by *self-interest* without concern for any ethics. Since many environmental effects are long term, they will not affect you and me during our lifetimes anyway, so why should we worry? A slightly different reaction is *self-protection*. We act to protect ourselves and our own families from the impact; with enough money we can pay more for scarce resources, or we can move to a less polluted country. A different reaction is that we are simply *overwhelmed* by the whole issue; it is too difficult to cope with or even think about. This may take the form of *denial*, where the information is treated as untrue or badly exaggerated. Another form of the 'overwhelmed' reaction is *fatalism* where we decide we can't do anything about it anyway so may as well just carry on as we are. Another reaction is what some ecologists have called *'sidestepping'*. This means doing something positive to mitigate the environmental costs of our lifestyles without otherwise changing those lifestyles. A recent and large-scale form of this is carbon emission offsetting (obtaining carbon credits) especially for air travel.

III. The Christian Creator God

Christians are engaged in Earth spiritualities along with members of other religious faiths, those with no religion, and those for whom the green movement is an alternative to traditional forms of religion. The classic Christian creeds begin 'I/we believe in God . . . Creator of heaven and earth'. We might expect then that Christians would have deep respect for God's creation. Yet Christian communities seem to be no less vandalistic toward their natural environment than anyone else.

An attitude to other Earth beings that regarded them as utilities may have seemed natural to those human beings who saw themselves as superiors and masters of everything else. There was still the problem of God, though! To be consistent, such an unconstrained view of human power to exploit required the elimination of God as creator, so that the most powerful human beings were answerable to no one else, or it required a God who was loving and forgiving toward human beings no matter what they did, or it required a God who wanted some human beings to be powerful managers dominating everyone and everything else in the name of that God. Various branches of Christian theology were able to supply these requirements. Secular theology simply eliminated God and left humans in charge of everything. A personalist theology provided a God who was all-loving and all-forgiving toward human beings, a favouritism with which no other species, eco-system or Earth-process could compete. A more industrial theology, on the other hand, provided a God who favoured hard work and delivered the rest of the planet into human hands as raw material.

IV. Key concepts in Christian Earth spirituality

Although Christian theology has supplied, often unintentionally, some of the motivation to support a dominating human attitude to the rest to the planet Earth, there are also key concepts in Christianity that contest such dominance and support a Christian attitude of respect and care for those other Earth beings and processes with which and within which we interact. One of these is the idea of the 'sacramentality' of all things, which sees all created realities as embodiment of the divine and a resource for knowledge of and intimacy with their Creator.[3] Every created being has its own value, which derives from its divine creator irrespective of any use it may have to human beings. A second such traditional concept derives from 'eschatology' when this is understood as a future-oriented view of the cosmos on a journey toward fulfilment in God of which humans are a part.[4] The future is at least as valuable as the present. Some other important concepts are extensions of established concepts in social justice. Thus, the idea of working for justice for *all people* (rather than just my own friends, colleagues, and family) extends to become justice for *all living creatures*. The goal of the *common good* of all nations (rather than just my own nation) becomes the planetary good of *all the beings and processes* that constitute the planet Earth. The goal of the *development* (social, economic, political) of nations becomes that of *sustainable sufficiency*, which means equity among people living within the regenerative capacities of Earth. And *solidarity* with *marginalized people* (rather than treating everyone the same regardless of existing inequities) becomes solidarity with the most *vulnerable species*.[5] Along with these older familiar concepts, contemporary Christian spirituality has had to adopt new concepts from other disciplines. Among these are the concepts of 'eco-system', 'intrinsic value', and 'sustainability'. All of these have resonances with traditional Christian theology but have added detail and centrality to those older understandings. To these we may add 'eco-justice' which requires a combination of justice among human beings with respect for Earth's non-human beings, processes, and eco-systems.

V. Christian theology back to its roots

At the biblical roots of Christianity we find a respect for a Creator God and attitudes to both Creator and creation that are summed up in the beatitudes (Matt. 5.1–12). The beatitudes express a spirituality that is centred on God and embodied in relationships with God's creation. We have most commonly understood the spirituality of the beatitudes as embodied in our relationships with other human beings: blessings on the poor in spirit, those who mourn, the meek, those who hunger and thirst for justice, the pure in heart, the peacemakers, and the persecuted.[6] Just as easily, they summarize how we relate to God through the whole world around us, not just the human beings within it. They are blessings on those whose spirit of voluntary poverty does not seek to consume and possess, who grieve for lost species and destroyed eco-systems, who walk gently rather than vandalistically within the Earth, who seek right relationships with other beings, whose pure hearts allow a clarity of vision about the state of the world, who live peacefully with minimal violence to any other being, and who maintain integrity in spite of persecution or ridicule.

The beatitudes are not of course the only way of summarizing this centre of Christian Earth spirituality. The key Christian beliefs in our active participation in *the reign of God* in our world and the *resurrection* also provide a basis for an Earth spirituality that is not exploitative and wasteful. The reign of God is not only about just and peaceful relationships among human beings but includes the wider cosmos extending beyond human relationships. The resurrection of our bodies is a central belief that ties us both individually and as a species into the future of the planet Earth as our continuing bodily abode. Both these key beliefs direct us spiritually and ethically to participation in the Earth rather than domination of Earth or an eventual release from it.

VI. Asceticism

Rather than a leader in the movement toward environmental sustainability, Christian theology has on the whole been a learner from environment sciences and public movements. Theology may need to continue to be sensitive to advances in such movements that cue us into needed changes in ways of attending theologically and spiritually to the world in which we live.

One such recent cue comes from the 'new thrift' as a reaction to the economic costs of climate change and diminishing energy resources. Much of this now popular advocacy for restraint on consumerism may seem crass and self-serving, too late and too little. The more cynical commentators have pointed out that peoples' first choices will be the easiest ones. A budget-conscious lifestyle can be good for the wallet and is mostly, but not always, good for the environment. Saving money and more ethical choices do not always go hand in hand. Cheaper eggs from caged hens may win out over free-range eggs.

But two aspects of this new thrift should lead us to take it more seriously. One is that this is a plausible public argument readily communicable on a wide scale. In the end it is the public support for environmental sustainability that will have real public effects. It is public support also that will allow democratic governments to implement environmental policies. A second aspect is that the idea of 'thrift' points us to the idea of self-discipline. It reminds us of the importance of self-discipline in many walks of life such as the strong contemporary emphasis on self-discipline in sport, in international peace-keeping, and in an education system that requires self-denial for the sake of deferred goals. It also reminds us of the tradition of Christian asceticism,[7] which has diminished in recent Christian consciousness in favour of spiritualities that emphasize more immediately positive attitudes such as celebration and the goodness of life.

Asceticism has fallen into some disrepute recently in Christian spirituality because its practices have often come to be seen as a pathology. But it may also be seen positively today as something deep within the human spirit that is a requirement for all human endeavour.[8] Asceticism may be described as disciplined living for the sake of a greater good.[9] 'Disciple' and 'discipline' go together here. The term 'asceticism' implies an arduous physical or moral effort to attain a goal. And we could appropriately remember here that ascetics are the opposite of consumers and polluters. One of the influential biblical images for the Christian understanding of asceticism is Paul's comparison of his own spiritual life to the training undergone by athletes in order to obtain victory (1 Cor. 9.24–7).

Ascetical theology has usually been focused on the individual's journey to perfection. A contemporary Earth spirituality would probably not be focused so much on the individual. It would need nevertheless to retain the idea that respect for God's creation and a reformed human role within the Earth does require a change of mind and heart, an interior change within the human person. In its contemporary sense an ascetic spirituality involves a change of heart that is embodied in changes of lifestyle and especially changes from unsustainable patterns of consumption and production.

We may not want to use the term 'ascetic' to describe a contemporary Earth spirituality. 'Voluntary simplicity' or 'living simply' might communicate more easily in the contemporary world, but such gentler terms do seem to slide off the arduous and dedicated nature of the task. In any case, attention to the old asceticism reminds us that the struggle is not all out there. It is also within us. For people living in consumer societies, that struggle is chiefly a negative one of self-restraint in opposition to accepted patterns of consumption. On the positive side it involves contemporary virtuous practices such as reduce–re-use–recycle, being energy wise, protecting biodiversity, and conserving wilderness.

These are just contemporary ways of practising the beatitudes with a new sensitivity toward an environment now more threatened by us than it was before and requiring our focused attention. The tradition of asceticism focuses that attention on combating the destructive side of human life, which for several decades has received less attention in Christian spirituality than it did in the past.

We could hope, though, that an Earth spirituality that draws upon Christian spiritual resources of asceticism could play a positive part in environmental politics on the large scale of encouraging those in government or large corporations to adopt policies of sustainability. And perhaps even more so of encouraging the sense that even small things count. Small energy-wise or consumption-reducing or conservation-minded actions by a lot of people can make a difference not only to the immediate environment but also to the large-scale politics that are dependent on public opinion, public example, and the micro-politics of talking to neighbours and friends. This kind of spirituality is also now served by numerous websites that give advice on energy-saving, conservation, and eco-friendly lifestyles.

Concluding with conviviality

My intention in this article has been to promote the idea that Christian theology is well placed to contribute to the change of mind and heart that is being called for by contemporary ecology. This assumes, though, that we are able to direct our theology toward the public forum rather than see it as just personal or an affair internal to the Church or academia. It also assumes that we can draw positively on Christian traditions of asceticism in a way that does not simply repeat their practices, especially not those that now seem pathological, but that encourages the restraints inherent in a respectful human role in the planet Earth.

Lest we be too focused on the particular and lose the sense of the whole, let me conclude this article with a note on conviviality. Asceticism is only part of a larger spirituality of respect and care. Asceticism is not a means in itself but has commonly been understood as a path toward contemplation. In a more public and contemporary spirituality we could express that as a path toward conviviality, that is, the continuing human involvement in the exuberance of life in the Earth.

An Earth spirituality that calls our attention to asceticism and restraint is not meant to be doleful. Like voluntary poverty it is not meant to be sad. Even in its secular form the 'new thrift' with its constraints on spending need not feel like a 'sacrifice' any more than is the graffiti writer or the cigarette smoker's sense of loss when they decide to stop. This is the kind of restraint that allows focus on the emergence of the good, the healthy, and the beautiful. It promotes a sense of liberation from addictions and consumer attitudes that now appear as mental and emotional chains. The new asceticism opens new possibilities for conviviality that do not require possession or consumption. By giving up the pursuit of many trivial satisfactions we are able to pursue those few things that are most valuable to us, most of which can only be enjoyed and admired, not possessed or consumed.

Notes

1. The term thus covers a wide range of approaches as, for example, Navdany's vision of an earth democracy, www.navdanya.org; the plea of biological science to religion such as in E. O. Wilson, *Creation: An Appeal to Save Life on Earth*, New York and London: W. W. Norton, 2006; ecological spiritualities such as Ursula King, 'One Planet, One Spirit: Searching for an Ecologically Balanced Spirituality,' *Ecotheology* 10, no. 1 (2005): 66–87; ecological ethics such as Patrick Curry, *Ecological Ethics: An Introduction*, Cambridge: Polity Press, 2006; the policies of 'green' political parties; as well as the now extensive literature of eco-theology

2. One of the most prolific promoters of Christian theology's engagement in the public forum is Sean McDonagh. See, for example, his *Climate Change: The Challenge to All of Us*, Dublin: Columba Press, 2006.

3. Within Christian spirituality, examples may be found in such literature as Mary C. Grey, *Sacred Longings: Ecofeminist Theology and Globalization*, London: SCM Press, 2003; Denis Edwards, *Ecology at the Heart of Faith*, Maryknoll, NY: Orbis Books, 2006; and Norman Wirzba, *The Paradise of God: Renewing Religion in an Ecological Age*, Oxford: Oxford University Press, 2003.

4. An idea recently and extensively explored in John Hart, *Sacramental Commons: Christian Ecological Ethics*, Lanham, Md: Rowman & Littlefield, 2007.

5. An early example is John F. Haught, *The Promise of Nature: Ecology and Cosmic Purpose*, Mahwah, NJ: Paulist Press, 1993. Or more recently, Richard Woods, 'The Seven Bowls of Wrath: The Ecological Relevance of Revelation', *Biblical Theology Bulletin* 38, no. 2 (2007): 64–75.

6. This process of extension has been succinctly described in James Malone, 'Environmental Degradation and Social Justice,' *Origins* 22 (1993): 686–94.

7. Consider, for example, Brendan Byrne, 'The Beatitudes and "Poverty of Spirit" in the Ignatian Exercises', *The Way* 47, no. 1–2 (2008): 29–46.

8. The traditions, for example, of Celtic asceticism, of Francis and Clare of Assisi, or of the Spanish mysticism of Teresa of Avila and John of the Cross.

9. As, for example, in the recent entire issue of *Cross Currents* dedicated to 'Asceticism Today,' *Cross Currents* 57, no. 4 (2008).

10. Or in a more traditional terminology, the term asceticism designates the efforts of the Christian soul struggling to acquire perfection. Cf. Adolphe Tanquerey, *The Spiritual Life: A Treatise on Ascetical and Mystical Theology* (Tournai: Desclee & Co., *c.*1930).

Latin American Women: 'We are leaving behind patriarchal constructs and pushing toward something new'

I am an eco-feminist theologian who has been working in Chile in the area of eco-feminist theology, spirituality, and ethics since 1991. I am a founding member of two women's organizations here: *Con-spirando*, a women's collective that publishes a journal from an eco-feminist perspective (*Con-spirando: Revista latinoamericana de ecofeminismo, espiritualidad y teología*), and *Capacitar-Chile*, a team of women dedicated to holistic health and spirituality.[1] Women from these two teams come together every year to offer a School on Eco-feminist Spirituality and Ethics for activist women leaders throughout Latin America, most of whom have some theological formation. In this article, I propose to outline the process of these Schools and the ways they have developed women's eco-feminist consciousness and communities of faith.

What brought both groups together a decade and a half ago was our search for a spirituality that would water our souls as we struggled for a more just and humane world. All of us were feminists: some of us were grassroots organizers and Paulo Freire-taught popular educators, others were working in our churches and *comunidades de base* in programmes dealing with women, still others were teaching gender studies at local universities. We were searching for spiritual practices that were embodied, experiential, contextual. We needed to start from our own bodies, celebrating our own rites of passages and life cycles – and from there connect to other women who were engaged in a similar search. As we look back on our beginnings, there is no doubt that we were thirsting for new ways of celebrating together who we really were as humans: we were yearning for new ways of forming community, a new cosmology, a new theology and ethics, new stories of origin, new images of the sacred – in short, a new paradigm of meaning that moved

86

beyond the depressing constraints of patriarchy we had unconsciously made our own. We began describing this spirituality as *eco-feminist*.

In 1992, the *Con-spirando* collective invited women throughout Latin America to form a network. The first issue of our journal (March, 1992) expresses the goals of the network in this way: '[it] contributes to the creation of a culture that allows theological reflection and spirituality to flow from the rich diversity of our bodies, our communities, and the Earth itself. We call for cosmologies that question anthropocentrism and that expose relationships based on dominance of one class, ethnic group, gender, age, or sexual orientation over another and of the human over other forms of life. Such cosmologies will have profound political consequences. This eco-feminist perspective unmasks the hierarchies in which we live and points toward a more holistic vision of our inter-relatedness. It is within this perspective that we seek a spirituality that will both heal and liberate. To do this, we need to *con-spirar juntas* – a phrase that attempts to convoke the image of the planet as a living, breathing organism to which we are all intrinsically linked in one great but myriad breath of life.'

Over the years, both teams have come to embrace the following commitments:

- Belief in the wisdom of our bodies and the priority of knowing through our corporeality in relationship. Intuition becomes a way of knowing;
- Efforts to search for non-hierarchical ways of being that model 'power with' rather than 'power over';
- Sharing new ways to celebrate and developing new rituals that nurture our spiritualities and commitments;
- Re-examining those foundational myths on which Western Christian culture is based in order to relativize them and to search for other myths – especially those of our indigenous ancestors – that support our emerging spiritualities, theologies, and ethics;
- Promoting an eco-feminist ethic of sustainability that moves toward interconnectedness with the entire Earth community.

Both teams have tried to put these commitments into practice in circular fashion: our workshops, summer schools, educational modules, rituals, discussion groups, and seminars water our publications and our web page and are watered by them, all forging a network of Latin American women engaged with each other and with the great issues of our times. These women constitute an emerging cadre of leaders whose style is much more intuitive, more relational – and therefore, we believe, more effective in bringing about the cultural change so desired at this time in history.

Early on, both the *Con-spirando* and *Capacitar* teams realized that if we were to find the commitment and enthusiasm to stop destroying the planet, we would have to change our theological concepts of both God and the human. We would have to re-examine our images of the sacred and our myths about where we came from, our purpose, and where we were going. One of the ways in which we have sought to do this has been through an annual Summer School.

I. School of Eco-feminist Spirituality and Ethics

I should like to describe the summer school process in more detail, because it is a microcosm of what we are trying to accomplish. Starting in 2000, women from both teams joined together to organize our *School of Eco-feminist Spirituality and Ethics*, which brings together approximately forty activist women leaders from Latin America annually. This initiative grew out of an earlier project called 'Shared Garden', co-sponsored by *Con-spirando* in Chile, the eco-feminist theologian Ivone Gebara in Brazil, and feminist theologians Mary Hunt and Diann Neu of WATER in the United States. It was during the Shared Garden process that the theme of myths and their power over us first surfaced. Participants enacted and then analyzed the creation story of Adam and Eve as found in Genesis 2, the foundational myth undergirding our current patriarchal Christian culture. It was during this process that we began to realize how much we have internalized this myth – which sustains both our cultures and our cosmologies – and continues to operate within us at a very deep, although frequently unconscious level.

Our recognition of the need to delve more deeply into how myths originate as well as how they can operate to uphold patriarchy as normal or God-given led to our commitment to hold an annual summer school. This school would offer, for ten brief days, a contained space and time where women could ask their theological questions without fear. It would be a safe space allowing participants to search together for more life-giving theologies, cosmologies, and ways of celebrating our emerging spiritualities. It would be a space to search together and formulate our own body of thought, study, and reflection as Latin American women engaged in the religious debates of our region.

The team was convinced that, as a first step, it would be key for women in Latin America to deepen both our analysis and our theoretical deconstruction of both the Genesis myth and myths in general to be able to see how they act in our sub-consciousness, determining how they affect the way we relate to one another. At the same time, we were convinced that we needed to begin to build new practices and power relations as we looked for ways to sustain ourselves in terms of constructs of meaning both at the personal and at the communal level. This entailed searching for new stories of meaning, new myths and rituals.

During our first school our central theme was 'Myths and their power over us', and we began the all-important process of deconstruction. During that school in January 2000, we developed our own understanding of myth based on our own experiences, looking especially hard at those myths dealing with women's bodies, how they evolved in the human psyche, as well as in an individual woman's life-cycle. We analyzed both our cultural and psychological need for myth and how we might transform myths and use their power over us to empower ourselves. We honed in on the four basic archetypes that shape us as women – Mother/Life-giver; Lover/Companion; Amazon/ Warrior; Wise Woman/Medium – and saw these archetypes reflected in the many goddesses who have appeared throughout the ages.

Because both participants and the team found these themes to be so gripping for their lives, 'Myths and their power over us II' was unanimously chosen as the central theme for our second school, held in January 2001. We concentrated specifically on the four feminine archetypes as developed by Toni Wolff, close collaborator of Carl Jung. Two Jungian psychologists, both experts in the work of Toni Wolff, have accompanied us during the schools: first, Dr Madonna Kolbenschlag, who died suddenly at the end of the first school in 2000, then by Dr Rachel Fitzgerald who continues to help us deepen our knowledge of the archetypes from an eco-feminist perspective.

Based on the evaluations of participants and facilitators, the team chose to stay with this theme for our third school, held in January 2002, but this time to concentrate on the shadow side of each of the four archetypes and to examine the process of stereotyping the original energy of each. This included the many ethical norms related to women and our bodies developed over time, as the patriarchal perspective came to be the norm. Thus, the theme for the third School was 'Myths and Power III: Women's Bodies – Ethical Implications.

A significant new insight that has emerged for us is that it is possible to situate the Christian myth within the broader sweep of our evolution as a species and to gain a much larger sense of the history of the universe and of the antiquity of our roots. Part of this process is to rediscover the femi-

nine images of the Divine,[3] still present among our indigenous peoples as
Pachamama, Earth Mother. When the feminine is not present, honoured in
ritual[4] or in a culture's sacred image of the Divine, the entire social fabric is
affected, and violence against women becomes commonplace.

Through the summer schools, we have learned that the starting point of
eco-feminist methodology is a commitment to embodied learning – listening to our own bodies, the bodies of our abused sisters, the Earth Body. This
includes staying profoundly connected to dreams, intuitions, emotions, sen-
sations, and the wisdom found in women's rituals. Those of us engaged in
this process are committed to accepting our differences, remaining flexible
and refusing rigid postures. We take seriously the responsibility to continue
educating ourselves and to work toward building links of solidarity among
ourselves. Empowering each other and making more visible our network are
major goals.

II. Working toward a post-patriarchal paradigm

Out of the network emerging from the school, there is evolving a new anthropology (the way we now understand ourselves as humans), a new cosmology
(our understanding of our origins, which in turn has altered our images of
the Sacred) and a new epistemology (the sources for our knowledge). This
shifting affects our ethical postures and our spiritual practices and is evident
in the witness given by a number of women who have participated in the
school. During 2001–2002, I interviewed a sampling of such women from
ten different Latin American countries who had been involved in the liberation theology movements in the region and who today are working in
feminist theology.[5]

In a variety of ways, the women interviewed express a shift in their understanding of *who we are as humans*. Their sense of themselves as individual,
separate egos is evolving toward a larger sense of self. We humans are not
superior to the rest of the life community; we are part of the natural world,
part of the materiality of the universe – or as Agamedilza from Manaus,
in Brazil's Amazon, reminds us, we are brothers and sisters of Nature.
'Everything that happens to the Earth, happens to me,' reflects Silvia from
Costa Rica. Referring to her own struggle with breast cancer, she says: 'My
sick body is also related to the Earth's devastation.' Alcira from Bolivia
speaks of her own internal eco-system as a mirror image of the external eco-
system where she lives, and knows that she must live in reciprocity with both
because each depends on the other.

Some of the women spoke of themselves as 'beings in process,' as incomplete in themselves yet linked to all those who have gone before them and to all those who will come after. More than anything else, these women are finding a deep sense of belonging – of intimacy and participation – with the Earth and the entire Cosmos. The shift taking place is this: we recognize that we belong to a larger, greater self than our current flesh and bones configuration. Indigenous peoples have always known this intuitively; the new science is now telling us the same thing empirically. Everything is related to everything else and nothing is independent. We are one interconnected web with all and in all.

The *god-images* of these women are clearly shifting from a deity outside and above the created universe to a sense of something within yet beyond; a relationship that holds everything together. To describe this changing view of their god-images, they used words such as Energy, Presence, Wisdom, Matrix, Complementarity, Memory, Intuitive Space, Greater Reality, Envelopment, Fountain of Life. All talked of *experiencing* this energy rather than being able to define it.

Marcia from Ecuador says, 'For me, God is not all-powerful, but rather something that goes beyond the imaginable, something that needs to be discovered at every moment of our existence; it is there where the human-divine mystery is found, because both are, in the end, mystery.' God is the impulse for my body, the strength of my thoughts, the container for my feelings, and the energy behind all that I am creating. God is all the vitality I find in both people and in nature.'

According to Coca from Argentina, 'Contact with nature, just as contact with other people, contact with tenderness as well as with pain – these speak to me of an Existence that encircles us and at the same time has something to do with fluidity.' Alcira says, 'I understand and feel the Sacred as an experience of energy, which is a more open image. It is an energy that is here, in me, in the trees, the animals, in relationship, in the ways we love, the way we live out our commitments. This energy is Sacred; you find it and experience it through many symbols and names, rituals and myths, in relation with others. This energy, which I call Divine or Sacred Energy, is circular. It is like a current that flows and infuses life: this energy makes all life blossom forth and grow.'

Doris from Chile says, 'There is not outside/inside or up/down: all is part of the Sacred. Thus life is sacred, our bodies are sacred: that is why we must struggle to end torture, violence against women and children, hunger and cold for the millions of marginalized people. All are in God, all are sacred – as are the rivers, which are the Earth's bloodstream, and if they are contaminated death will circulate throughout the whole body.'

The shift taking place in cosmology is nowhere more evident than in the interviewees' *beliefs about death and resurrection*. The majority view death and life not as separate, but as part of the same cycle. They speak of returning to that primal energy, that original goodness from which they came. Most reflected a deep peace about returning to this matrix, to being dissolved into the Earth as a coming home. As Gladys from Venezuela says, 'When I die, I will return to my place of origin and I confide in that original goodness.' Some of these women have lost parents recently and spoke of how the deaths of these loved ones have convinced them that a deep connection continues. They speak of memory – how those dearly loved are present in the memories we have of them.

Silvia, who is deeply involved in her Brazilian-Afro religious roots, puts it this way: the Brazilian-Afro religions have this dimension of community – that we are more than what we are now in our bodies. 'Those of us who are here form a community, but those who have gone on are also members of this community. Those who die become ancestors and communicate energy to us. That is what ancestrality means to me: the continuation of a life, of a mission. Positive energy and power never die. These ancestors will continue in nature as rocks or rivers, etc. For Afro religions these people really do become immortal in that they become a permanent presence in a place in nature. Thus their histories stay with us forever and the person is more present to us than absent.' These loved ones live on in our gene pool, in the very characteristics that make us kin – a certain laugh, a way of walking, a gesture. As Alcira puts it in describing her mother: 'She is alive in all those kind ways she marked my life. It is based on this experience that I can say that I have felt resurrection in life. She is present in the music she liked, the food she cooked, all the advice she gave me over the years, in the garden she planted.'

Nowhere is the shift to a post-patriarchal way of being more visible than in the way the women interviewed perceive, or know (*epistemology*). The body and bodily experience become the locus for understanding, for feeling both pleasure and pain, for judging right and wrong. The body – not in the abstract, but in our women's sexual, sensual, abused and wounded bodies – is where these women are weaving their cosmologies and theologies, their ethics and their spiritual practices. This emphasis on the body is clearly a reaction to millennia of patriarchal oppression, in which women's bodies were seen as property to be used and dominated as a receptacle to reproduce the species, and to centuries of Judeo-Christian teaching, in which women were seen as the cause of humanity's Fall from grace and thus the font of evil, temptation, and concupiscence. Thus, much of feminist and eco-feminist insistence that we do theology from the body is an angry reaction to layers of patriarchal domination and a burning desire to cut through all the dualisms that split mind, spirit, and the soul from the body. Not just the women I interviewed, but multitudes of women throughout Latin America are reclaiming their bodies as sacred, as a source of holiness. This emphasis is righting a long-overdue imbalance where men/mind/spirit were considered superior to women/body/materiality.

The women all called for a *new ethics* based on the experiences of their own bodies, with all their accumulated history, wisdom, and longings. Starting from the body, then, is essential. And because ethical decisions will be made based on one's own experience, they will be contextualized, pluralistic and respectful of diversity.

Nothing captures the shift more than the way women are nurturing their evolving intuitions about who they are and what they perceive life's meaning to be. Most are no longer very nourished by the liturgies and worship services offered by their Churches. Yet while participation in official church worship wanes, a veritable boom in *women's rituals and celebrations* is taking place all over Latin America – and most of the women in our network are actively involved both in creating, convoking, and participating in these celebrations. The hallmark of these rituals is celebrating with one's whole body – through movement and dance.

What is being celebrated? Life – their own lives, the lives of loved ones, of other women, of those suffering, the lives of their ancestors; connection – to each other, to their own bio-region, to the seasonal cycles, to the elements, to the Earth itself and to the entire Cosmos; dreams – their own, the community's, the planet's. Many of these rituals are inspired by indigenous cosmologies. The remarkable creativity present in these rituals appears to have released a bottled-up longing to get out of our heads and celebrate freely with our entire bodies.

These women are also nurturing their spirituality through the practice of contemplation and meditation. They have moved on from traditional forms of meditation, although some still reflect on biblical passages. The great shift here is that all now turn to the natural world to find their peace, to renew their beings. Gladys climbs Mount Avila – a mountain on the outskirts of Caracas – everyday. Alcira has an uncanny relationship with trees and communes with them throughout the seasons. Doris and Coca do body movement such as Tai Chi to connect with the Cosmos. Graciela (Uruguay) gardens. Sandra paints, colours, and takes photos of Nature. Contact with sensuality – poetry, color, music – as well as with the pain of others, is also an essential element in this evolving spirituality.

Another source of spirituality is friendship and community – spaces for sharing heart-joys and heart-sorrows. Circles of women are sprouting up everywhere and have become spaces of freedom and healing. Sandra's experience is common: 'My feminist theology collective [in north-eastern Brazil] is a fundamental source of sustenance for me. Together we cultivate seeds of new beliefs and values for ourselves. This is our space, the place where we can feel accepted, where we can think, share, and celebrate together. The Sacred for me takes place in sharing, in sharing our experiences with others who also share their life journeys. In these moments, I know I am not alone.'

Conclusion

That we are leaving behind patriarchal constructs and pushing toward something new – yet something that we only intuit and cannot yet define – is clearly evident. We find ourselves at the beginning of a new common creation that is both exciting and daunting. As we embark on the long psychic journey of ridding ourselves and our world of a patriarchal mindset so imbedded in us that it seems as normal as the air we breathe, we have only faint glimmers of what a post-patriarchal world might look like. We have only intuitions, dreams, hunches – and a growing circle of like-minded seekers, each of whom now knows that she is not alone in her search.

Notes

1. *Capacitar-Chile* is part of a larger network of healers working in areas of conflict and poverty in five continents, cf. www.capacitar.org.
2. The team continues to offer schools and retreats on *Myths, Goddesses and Archetypes*.
3. Ritual has been a key ingredient in the schools: enacting the Sumerian myth of Inanna, walking the labyrinth, and many others.
4. This study was the subject of my doctoral thesis. M. J. Ress, *Ecofeminism in Latin America*, Maryknoll, NY: Orbis Books, 2006,

Learning from the Earth: Reflections on Theological Education and the Ecological Crisis

JOHN CLAMMER

The ecological crisis that now threatens the future of life on earth is not only a failure of the process of modernization with its goals of growth, industrialization, and urbanization upon which almost all the societies of our planet have pinned their hopes, but is also a failure of the imagination. Talk of the crisis being at its root a spiritual one, while no doubt accurate in its way, conceals the fact that spirituality itself is socially located, and the forms that it takes are deeply influenced by the culture of which it is an expression, and of which education is a significant part. A failure of the imagination is thus to a great extent a failure of education – to inform, to foresee, to analyze, and to prepare the next generation for the challenges that confront it. An argument can be made that this failure to understand and embody the deep structures of change in the contemporary world applies as much to theological education as it does to its secular varieties, perhaps even more so, as while theological education should be concerned with the fundamental nature of being and reality, and secular education more with the mechanics of empirical processes, in fact it has been the latter through such media as environmental studies and development studies that have been closer to naming and responding to the true nature of the issues that, through our myopia or greed, now confront not only the entire human family, but equally all the other inhabitants of the total biosphere that we call the Earth, this remarkable and fragile gift that we have been entrusted with and have so systematically abused.

The rather belated discovery by theologians and by activists and analysts of many faiths of both the extent of the ecological crisis and of potential resources within their faith traditions for addressing these problems has led to a rapidly growing literature (for a tiny sampling see Gottleib 2004, Hessel 1996, Ruether 1994, Kaza and Kraft 2000). For the most part however this literature does not address the question of theological education or the critical question of the extent to which that education should, in our current era, be rooted in, as it were, the earth rather than the heavens.

The present state of the world however testifies to the failure of the processes of modernization and 'development' to which we have become addicted and of the civilization that underlies and has generated our current systemic crisis, in which environmental degradation is only one part of a much bigger and holistic tragedy – of resource depletion, hugely unacceptable levels of poverty coexisting with runaway consumption in the rich nations, high levels of social injustice and social exclusion, war, conflicts and militarization, massive corruption, and the erosion of the cultural and religious worldviews that in the past underpinned our relationships to the natural world, our management of collective resources, and our economic relationships. The role of religion in all this has been ambiguous – a source of exploitative relationships to nature and to one another on the one hand, the fundamental source of ethics and ways of being-in-the-world on the other. Some would argue, and I would agree, that the weakest point for religion in the world (the context in which it must invariably operate) is praxis – the linking organically of faith and action, the derivation from faith of practices that transform and sustain the world and do so always against the acid test of practice itself – and its promotion of justice, both social and ecological.

The question then must inevitably arise of the adequacy of conventional education, both theological and secular, for addressing the unprecedented challenges that the global social, cultural, economic, and ecological spheres now confront us with in an absolutely unavoidable way. We might indeed argue that not only has conventional theological education proved inadequate to the task but that it has not even for the most part incorporated these pressing questions into its curriculum or teaching and learning methods. Preparing people to function in what is clearly a deeply dysfunctional social and global order is clearly 'old mind' thinking that entirely fails to address the new issues that the old paradigm has so negligently ignored (Ornstein and Ehrlich 1991). Any theologically trained person, whether in a pastoral role, teaching, writing, research, by the very nature of that discipline should be amongst the most alert to the contemporary groaning of the universe. This high calling of the theologian urgently invites us to consider the necessity of rethinking the nature of our educational institutions and their pedagogical methods to provide the necessary training, analytical skills, intellectual, practical, and imaginative resources necessary to confront the magnitude of the forces ranged against the creation of a secure and fulfilled humanity living in a sustainable and creative relationship with our natural environment, an environment that from a theological perspective represents the creativity and artistry of God, not simply the context in which human activity can be autonomously carried out.

If, as an imaginative exercise, we ask ourselves what this alternative education might be like, what would the answer be? I think that the starting point must be the observations made by the eco-theologian Thomas Berry about what he terms, in a powerful book of that name, 'The Great Work'. In the preface to that book Berry says:

> Of the institutions that should be guiding us into a viable future, the university has a special place because it teaches all those professions that guide the human endeavour. In recent centuries the universities have supported the exploitation of the Earth by their teaching in the various professions in the sciences, in engineering, law, education and economics. Only in literature, poetry, music, art, and occasionally in religion and the biological sciences, has the natural world received the care that it deserves. Our educational institutions need to see their purpose not as training personnel for exploiting the Earth, but as guiding students towards an intimate relationship with the Earth. For it is the planet itself that brings us into being, sustains us in life, and delights us with its wonders. In this context we must consider the intellectual, political and economic orientations that will enable us to fulfil the historical assignment before us – to establish a more viable way into the future (Berry 1999: x).

This implies of course that not only does theology involve the political, economic, and sociological but also that it involves a deep sense of what some are now calling 'Eco-Spirituality', an awareness of the magnificence and fragility of the cosmos, and an awareness that it is from nature that we not only draw our physical sustenance, but also our deepest emotional and artistic satisfactions.

This new historical mandate is no longer a luxury but a necessity. As Berry elsewhere notes, 'What is clear is that the earth is mandating that the human community assume a responsibility never assigned to any previous generation' (Berry 1988: 47), and that education plays a key role in this – in creating visions rather than in training people for specialized technical roles. But whereas Berry and his collaborators stress the new sense of cosmology that science has now bequeathed to us (although it was noted a generation ago in a rather different and much more anthropocentric way by thinkers such as

Teilhard de Chardin) – the magnificence, antiquity, complexity and ever-evolving nature of the universe, Leonardo Boff rightly counsels that:

> Having a new cosmology is not enough. How are we to spread it and bring people to internalize it so as to aspire to new behaviors, nourish new dreams, and bolster a new kindness toward the Earth? That is certainly a pedagogical challenge. As the old paradigm that atomized human beings, isolated them, and set them against the universe and the community of living beings permeated through all our pores in our lives and created a collective subjectivity suited to its intuitions, so now the new paradigm must form new kinds of subjectivity and enter into all realms of life, society, the family, media, and educational institutions in order to shape a new planetary man and woman, in cosmic solidarity and in tune with the overall direction of the evolutionary process (Boff 1997: 119).

The implications of this are many and rich – a new eco-centered approach to education in general, a new role for theology and the most potentially integrative of all the disciplines, and an overcoming of the ancient dichotomies of sacred/secular, material/spiritual, body/spirit and development/ecology. The new holism announced by so called 'New Age' (but often in fact highly integral) thinkers such as Ken Wilbur (e.g. in his book *A Theory of Everything*, 2004) is actually the model of the universe that we now require, and it is one that actually dissolves the distinction between religious education and 'secular' education, since in a living, growing, creative universe in which, to use Rabbi David Cooper's phrase 'God is a Verb' (Cooper 1997), everything is equally sacred if our enhanced awareness allows us to see it as such. Such an awareness also points to what the development ethicist Denis Goulet calls 'integral authentic development', in which, while recognizing that the current threat to nature comes from what is usually termed 'development', the common opposition between that development (seen by Goulet and many others as, despite its many conceptual and practical problems, the main contemporary way of addressing what are actually the major moral issues of our day, including the persistence of massive world-wide poverty) on the one hand and ecology on the other must be overcome. This is because, essentially, issues of social justice and ecology are fundamentally linked, or as Goulet neatly puts it, 'There can be no sound development ethic without environmental wisdom and conversely, no environmental wisdom without a solid development ethic' (Goulet 1995: 119).

While in a secularized and globalized world in which many faiths contend for attention, as do the insidious demands of the consumerist culture of neo-liberal capitalism, theology (understood in its specifically Christian context) may well appear to have lost its status as 'Queen of the Sciences'. But perhaps not, since not only is (Christian) theology in a globalized and plural world necessarily forced to confront the reality of other faith traditions and to enter into dialogue with them, but it also remains, even today, the most integral of the disciplines, containing as it does history, linguistics, archeology, anthropology, textual criticism, sociology, psychology, and the applied dimensions of these fields in pastoral care, counselling, development and social work, as well as its specifically 'religious' dimensions and their expression in such areas as liturgy. With the rising perception that the roots of our current crisis are essentially spiritual, theology takes on a new salience, as witnessed by the numbers of students world-wide who enter the discipline with no intention of ever taking up a pastoral career. In a world in which new models of education are urgently needed, theology when informed and permeated by an Earth spirituality (the definition of which in a Christian context is itself a challenge and an adventure), stands poised to renew itself and as such to provide a renewing force in the wider world, far outside of the boundaries of the narrowly defined faith community.

   In discussing the nature of deep change – the fundamental shifts in consciousness and social and institutional organization that might lead us out of our present critical predicament – the authors of the remarkable collaborative volume *Presence: An Exploration of Profound Change in People, Organizations and Society* (Senge, Scharmer, Jaworski, and Flowers 2004) come to the conclusion that 'In the end, we conclude that understanding presence and the possibilities of larger fields for change can only come from many perspectives – from the emerging science of living systems, from the creative arts, from profound organizational change experiences, and from direct contact with the generative capacities of nature. Virtually all indigenous or native cultures have regarded nature or the universe or Mother Earth as the ultimate teacher. At few points in history has the need to rediscover this teacher been greater' (Senge, Scharmer, Jaworski and Flowers 2004: 14–15). Deep change springs from an acute awareness of the objective conditions of the world and its interconnected economic, political, social, and ecological processes, rooted in the appreciation of spirituality, psychology, and creativity, or as the authors of *Presence* put it 'science performed with the mind of wisdom'. This is indeed the education for integral development of which Edmund O'Sullivan speaks in his seminal volume *Transformative Learning* (O'Sullivan 1999) – an education that includes not only the traditional and denominational content of mainstream theological education but also and equally an emphasis on education for ecological awareness, quality of life in its fullest sense, including the enhancement of creativity and simplicity, the nurturing of spiritual discovery and development, encouraging an under-standing of the planetary context of life and its cosmic and evolutionary dimensions, and education for peace, justice, and diversity. This is what Jean Paul Lederach in his luminous book on peace and conflict resolution calls 'the moral imagination' – 'the capacity to imagine ourselves in a web of relationships that includes our enemies; the ability to sustain a paradoxical curiosity that embraces complexity without reliance on dualistic polarity; the fundamental belief in and pursuit of the creative act; and the acceptance of the inherent risk of stepping into the mystery of the unknown that lies beyond the far too familiar landscape of violence' (Lederach 2005: 5).

Thomas Berry, whom I have quoted extensively above, in challenging the nature of higher education, throws out a challenge to the universities in par-ticular: 'The universities must decide whether they will continue training persons for temporary survival in the declining Cenozoic Era or whether they will begin educating students for the emerging Ecozoic' (Berry 1999: 71). How theologians are responding to this challenge we see in this volume and in the burgeoning literature that is beginning seriously to address the interface between faith and the natural world. We have collectively moved to the point where we see that the ecological crisis is our biggest planetary challenge. As a non-theologian but as an individual who daily confronts the violence of development, the violence of contemporary culture and civiliza-tion to toward nature, toward one another, and in particular to the vulnerable in society, to women, children, the aged and the marginalized, I constantly see the need for an integral development – one that links the spiritual to the practical concerns of the created world, one that allows belief to speak not just words of hope but words of transformation to the desperately groaning world. The key to this is a form of education that itself has undergone 'con-version' from a manipulative and exploitative relationship to the sustaining Earth, to one in which that Earth itself becomes our teacher and the cradle of a new humanity and form of civilization. And it is theology, as the bridge between our deepest existential concerns and the world, that should be the theatre of enlightenment rather than the theatre of destruction and injustice, that holds that key in its hands if it can but redefine itself as an orientation to the Earth as our home and potentially as the Earthly paradise that is still the substance of our dreams and our utopias.

References

Berry, Thomas (1988). *The Dream of the Earth*. San Francisco: Sierra Club Books

Berry, Thomas (1999). *The Great Work*. New York: Bell Tower

Boff, Leonardo (1997). *Cry of the Earth, Cry of the Poor*. Maryknoll, NY: Orbis Books

Cooper, David A. (1997). *God is a Verb: Kabbalah and the Practice of Mystical Judaism*. New York: Riverhead Books

Gottlieb, Roger S. (2004). *This Sacred Earth: Religion, Nature, Environment*. London and New York: Routledge

Goulet, Denis (1995). *Development Ethics: A Guide to Theory and Practice*. New York: The Apex Press; London: Zed Books

Hessel, Dieter, T. (ed.) (1996). *Theology for Earth Community*. Maryknoll, NY: Orbis Books

Kaza, Stephanie and Kenneth Kraft, (eds.) (2000). *Dharma Rain: Sources of Buddhist Environmentalism*. Boston and London: Shambhala

Ornstein, Robert and Paul Ehrlich (1991). *New World New Mind: Changing the Way We Think to Change Our Future*. London: Paladin

O'Sullivan, Edmund (1999). *Transformative Learning: Educational Vision for the Twenty-first Century*. Toronto: University of Toronto Press and London and New York: Zed Books

Ruether, Rosemary Radford (1994). *Gaia and God: Ecofeminist Theology of Earth Healing*. San Francisco: HarperSanFrancisco

Senge, Peter, C. Otto Scharmer, Joseph Jaworski and Betty Sue Flowers (2004). *Presence: An Exploration of Profound Change in People, Organizations and Society*. New York

Wilbur, Ken (2004). A Theory of Everything: An Integral Vision for Business, Politics, Science and Spirituality. Dublin: Gateway

THEOLOGICAL FORUM

Theology and Ecology: Moltmann and Boff

JOSIAS DE COSTA JÚNIOR

The purpose of this contribution is to examine the relationship between theology and ecology through comparing the approaches of Jürgen Moltmann and Leonardo Boff. I set out to show what is specific to each and to consider epistemological approaches that underlie their contributions: contextuality, affectivity, and inclusivism.

The process of self-examination Christian theology has gone through, which involved accepting its association with patriarchal oppression and with a rigid monotheism that resulted in transcendentalism, also laid bare its anti-ecological stance. Today ecology is a challenge to theology, since it is an invitation for knowledge to be arranged in a different manner. Seeking to understand something that concerns us leads us into the field of epistemology.

The existing literature produced from an ecological viewpoint provides us with an extensive search for an interpretation of the proper way to approach the environment or to make 'good use of nature'.[1] This means that ecology has provided a critical challenge to the attitude of modern man. This critique implies a questioning of his anthropological and ethical presuppositions, thereby underpinning the emergence of a new paradigm.[2]

Christian theology has made both positive and negative contributions to building the paradigm of modern man, as characterized by technological development at the expense of nature, which is being impiously destroyed. This has turned theology into a target of critiques made of the relationship of human beings to nature.[3] In this sense, the relationship between theology and ecology is one of challenge, since the former faces the accusation of belonging to a tradition that has caused the destruction of the environment.

I. Liberation and ecology

The Brazilian theologian Leonardo Boff has undoubtedly been foremost in considering ecology within the theological context of Latin America. His most significant work on the subject attempts to articulate two cries: that of the oppressed with that of the Earth: 'The cry of the oppressed contains a powerful reflection directed at liberation practices.'⁴ Boff sees ecology as re-positioning liberation theology, meaning that liberation theology has to take in the new cosmology, which sees the world as 'a living super-organism linked to the whole universe in cosmogenesis'.⁵ He points out that modern theology has coined the expression 'panentheism', meaning that God is in everything without everything being God, which, he claims, is both a consequence and a deepening of contemporary cosmology. He allows himself to play on this new ecological cosmovision, which accentuates God's immanence, God's involvement in all processes without becoming lost in them.

Boff sets out an eco-spirituality linked to an eco-theology. In his panentheism, God is permanently present in his creation in a decisive fashion. God and the world are different, without being separated or closed off from one another. 'They are open one to the other. They find themselves always mutually implicated.'⁶ This separateness is in order for there to be communication and union through communion and mutual presence, which is transparency (*diaphany*), transparency in immanence. One implication of this outlook is the sacredness of all things, because God is present in every being and in its history.

Ecological discourse also makes it possible and reasonable to speak of God as a Trinity of Persons. The Trinity is an interplay of relationships: an ecological God. It is the ecological that produces the emergence of relational and 'communional' understanding of the divinity. God is communion and relationship, and this is why the universe exists in relationship and everything is in communion with everything. All the complexity, diversity, unity, intermingling, inter-relationship of the world is a reflection of the Trinity.⁷ Therefore, the Trinity is the expression of the ultimate reality: God.

In Boff's view, the cause and foundation of oppression in the Church and society is monotheism. This viewpoint makes his Trinitarian theology a quest to build a cosmic and ecological democracy. Concern to establish a scientific grounding for his theology, seeking a clear epistemological structure, with analytical and scientific theoretical instruments, is not in evidence. The 'new paradigm' makes mysticism its main emphasis, and this becomes the basis for the search for an ecological spirituality. He argues for a nexus between spirituality and ecology formed by cosmic mysticism.[8] This spirituality should lend a new meaning to life, which is connected to everything, to the whole universal reality, diverse and unified. It is therefore an ecological spirituality, the main outcome of which will be the re-enchantment of nature. Modern rationalism tried to exclude fantasy, desire, inventiveness, but on the lines indicated by Leonardo Boff's theology – and as suggested by Michel Maffesoli[9] – epistemology should be inclusive and affective.

II. Trinity and creation

For Jürgen Moltmann, Christian theology has only one concern: God.[10] Ecological theology should be the affirmation of a complex theoretical conceptual universe that seeks to learn about God and to move beyond theoretical concepts and edifices that think of God starting with power categories. It seeks to replace the monotheistic epistemology that emphasizes the divine absolute monarch, the aim of which is to construct a doctrine of God that looks to establish the sovereignty and lordship of God, concepts of God and of God's relationship to the world that, to some extent, contribute to strengthening the idea of the dominating human being.

Ecology is not the object of Moltmann's reflection, so it does not dilute his theological discourse, which is founded on eminently theological reference points and not on the new cosmology and the new physics, even though there is dialogue with them. He does not open God's hand as an object of theology. He looks into the theological traditions for an adequate concept to articulate the concept of God in such a way that God is always relational. Trinitarian doctrine provides a starting point for this theological reflection from an ecological perspective, and its underlying concept is *perichoresis*, the circularity of the divine life in the communion and unity of the three divine Persons. This concept enables us to move beyond hierarchical, subordinative, and authoritarian ideas of God in favour of relational, non-hierarchical knowledge. So God does relate to the world; God is in his creation. This way of God's relating to the world comes about in a dynamic circularity, in which God is important to the world, just as the world and its history are important to God.

Trinitarian perichoresis forms the theoretical foundation for an ecological understanding of creation. Here is the centre of the Trinitarian question in Moltmann, so that we have a re-reading of perichoresis based on tradition and issuing in a contextual Trinitarian theology. Perichoresis destroys the rigid hierarchical schemes of the order of creation like old parchments. There is one element that is fundamental in the circle of communion of the divine Persons: love. This communion opens out beyond the Trinitarian circle to include the whole of creation. Moltmann calls this integrating, inclusive, unifying communion of the triune God 'open Trinity'.[11] It is 'open' in the abundance of the 'love that provides creatures with the space for them to live their vitality and the open space for their development'.[12] What Moltmann does is to conceive each Person of the Trinity in movement within the others, so that space is reciprocally conceded: each Person is living space for the others. In this way, God is in the world as the world is in God. It is perichoresis that defines his ecological doctrine of creation.

Another fundamental aspect of the ecological doctrine of doctrine of creation is that which refers to the cosmic spirit and human knowledge. Open systems have different forms of organization and means of communication, from formless matter to living systems, from the earth's eco-system to the solar system, from our Milky Way to the galaxies of the universe. The organizational principles of the Spirit work on two levels: on the synchronic level, self-affirmation and integration; on the diachronic level, self-preservation and self-transcendence.[13] The Spirit shows a tendency to develop more complex open systems in symbiotic life-forms and in the evolution of life-forms.

This shows us that opting for ecology has clear epistemological implications, since a theory of creation from an ecological perspective strives to break with analytical thinking with its dichotomy between subject and object, struggling to plough a new furrow in the processes of acquiring knowledge.[14] This new way of thinking points to abandonment of reason's claim to copy the model of modern physics as a model of an exact science. This model has been questioned, and in the wake of this questioning Moltmann is suggesting that knowledge needs to be acquired in a participative and not a dominating manner.[15] The perspective opened up with a theory of creation showing these characteristics is that it is open to other rationalities that cannot be reduced solely to the instrumental reasoning that characterizes modern science. Finally, the method suggested by Moltmann brings the great challenge of embracing different rationalities, which include both scientific knowledge and wisdom.

Final considerations

From the viewpoint of modern rationality it is always doubtful to speak of a methodology of knowledge that uses the characteristics suggested by the two theologians examined above. Including categories such as wisdom, intuition, and affectivity always arouses interrogatives in speaking of method. But beginning to think in a different way requires a different approach to knowledge. Examining epistemology means seeking to inspire processes of transmitting knowledge and trying to interfere in the hierarchical structures of power that are reproduced in the foundations of society and of our knowledge.

As for the theologians discussed here, Leonardo Boff displays a more practical concern when he establishes a link between spirituality and ecology, whereas Jürgen Moltmann demonstrates concern on the theoretical and epistemological levels. What emerges is that Moltmann's specific contribution is the search for an effective theological discourse that can operate on the social and political levels in the face of ecological reality. Boff, for his part, uses the new cosmology as a platform on which to build his liberating theological discourse. Both, as I see it, employ a contextual epistemology, since they respond to the demands of the historical moment in which we live and develop their arguments on the basis of local contexts that connect to the global one. It is in evaluating the context that experiences and knowledge are confirmed, with an opening to wider associations of ideas.

Another aspect is the introduction of affectivity into the process of knowing. For more objective thinkers this causes great alarm, since affectivity is related to emotions, with the feelings we experience. What is in question is the affectivity that suggests the abandonment of clarity in determining the limits between subjectivity and objectivity, as well as opening the door to the universe of emotions as a source of knowledge. It is not a matter of abandoning reason but of saying that it cannot exist independently of other factors.

The third aspect I mentioned is inclusivism. Theology has to be inclusive in order to embrace the diversity of our experiences. Our experience of God is polysemic, polyphonic, polyglot, and inclusive. An inclusive epistemology speaks of reciprocal interdependence and avoids pretensions to dominance, since what we know is related to other forms of understanding. Besides this, it welcomes multiple experiences of different expressions in the search for unity.

The two theologians discussed here hold to the idea that we need to construct new ways of knowing that will, in some way, relate to the new cosmologies, the new cosmic visions. We need to move beyond dualistic and hierarchical divisions that still lurk in our ways of knowing. Finally, we need an inclusive, open, ecumenical theology, as Moltmann and Boff teach us, along with eco-feminists and process thinkers, whom space forbids consideration of here.

Translated by Paul Burns

Notes

1. Cf. C. Larrère, *Du bon usage de la nature. Pour une philosophie de l'environnement*, Paris: Aubier, 1997, pp. 16–17.
2. Understood here as a basic model that interrogates reality, following T. S. Kuhn, *The Structure of Scientific Revolutions*, Chicago: Chicago Univ. Press, 1962.
3. L. White, Jr, 'The Historical Roots of our Ecological Crisis', *Science* 155 (1997) 1203–7, places the responsibility for the destruction of nature on the Christian and Jewish traditions, based on the biblical text 'subdue it [the earth]' (Gen. 1.28).
4. L. Boff, *Ecologia: grito da terra, grito dos pobres*, Petrópolis: Vozes, 1995, (Eng, trans. by P. Berryman, *Cry of the Earth, Cry of the Poor*, Maryknoll, NY: Orbis, 1995). (Here n.e., Rio de Janeiro: Sextane, 2004, p. 11).
5. *Ibid.*, p, 157.
6. *Ibid.*, p. 210.
7. Cf. Boff, *Ecologia, mundialização, espiritualidade. A emergência de um novo paradigma*, São Paulo: Ática, 1993, pp. 49–50.
8. Cf. *ibid.*
9. M. Maffesoli, *Éloge de la raison sensible*, Paris, Éd. de la Table Ronde, 1995.
10. Cf. J. Moltmann, *Experiences in Theology*, London: SCM Press, 2000 (here Port. trans., 2004, p. 31).
11. Moltmann, *Trinity and the Kingdom of God*, London: SCM Press, 1981 (here Port. trans., 2000, pp. 106–7).
12. Moltmann, *Experiences* (here Port. trans., p. 268).
13. Moltmann, *God in Creation: An Ecological Doctrine of Creation*, London: SCM Press, 1985 (here Port. trans., p.10).
14. *Ibid.*, p. 2.
15. *Ibid.*, p. 2–4.

Sister Dorothy Stang: A Model of Holiness and Martyrdom

LUIZ CARLOS SUSIN

On 12 February 2005, a Saturday, the whole of Brazil was stunned by the news that Sr Dorothy Stang had been assassinated. The fact is that many Brazilians were only beginning to take notice of the existence and struggles of the diminutive Sister with her soft voice and broad smile, seventy-three years old. On that morning the gunmen contracted to get rid of her found her alone on a track in the middle of the Amazonian forest, carrying a New Testament and some papers containing instructions on the PDS (Sustainable Development Project) that she, together with other Sisters from her Congregation, was pursuing passionately in the depth of the forest. That morning Sr Dorothy, as was her wont, was on her way to see some families settled in the forest who were members of the PDS. When the armed youths blocked her way, she, who had already received death threats, saw the immediate danger and tried to engage them in conversation. She almost dissuaded them from killing her and even managed to read some verses from the Gospels to them, telling them that her weapon was that holy book. But the small price they had been offered counted for more, and six shots fired at point-blank range left her lying on her face on the ground in the emptiness of the forest. Then a tropical rainstorm came on, and her blood bathed the ground she had loved and defended. And so it was that, distraught and weeping with the forest, the families she had come to see found her later. Her lifeless body remained stretched out on the ground till late that evening, waiting for representatives of the law, while around her the people of the region and her Sisters in the Congregation held hands, wept, and prayed. This was the day that Amazonia lost a friend and gained an angel, in the words of Felício Pontes, Jr, a young Procurator of the Republic and colleague of Sr Dorothy in struggles on behalf of the peoples of the forest.

Why did they kill Sr Dorothy? Could she have been seen as a threat, at her advanced age, with her soft voice and wide smile? A clear explanation was given at the World Forum for Theology and Liberation, held in Belém, capital of the State of Pará, by Procurator Felício Pontes: Sr Dorothy was killed in the clash between two great projects affecting life and the economy, which are presently locked in a violent struggle in the State of Pará, which, together with that of Amazonas, contains the greatest area of Amazonian forest (which extends over half of Brazil, embracing eight States, as well as five other Latin American countries). More than any other part of Amazonia, Pará is now the front line forming, in the words of Marina da Silva, former Environment Minister of Brazil, the 'predatory frontier' of Amazonia.

On one side is the traditional way of life of the forest peoples, who live integrated into it, on the banks of its innumerable rivers, on their creeks and pools, or by the *igarapés* (false rivers): they derive their extractive economy from the forest and plant their crops and build their villages in its clearings. These are not just the indigenous peoples who keep their languages and cultures but, in far greater numbers, people of mixed race, simply Amazonian people. They have no titles to the lands of their ancestors; they are children of the land. On the other side is the agri-business project, concerned with exporting timber, minerals, meat, and soya. Its people are landowners with the power to fell the forest and install their huge tracts of monoculture and stock-raising. Exporting, in the current globalized economy, is clearly the means of earning most money, of amassing the greatest wealth. And agri-business provides Brazil's greatest source of exports. But this is taking place at the expense of the environment and of the people who live in the vastness of the country's interior. Sr Dorothy had predecessors: the clash between these two projects led to the death, in another area of the forest, of Chico Mendes, a union leader assassinated on the orders of powerful farmers in the region, as well as the deaths of the young priest Josimo Tavares, convenor of the Pastoral Land Commission, and of Sr Adelaide Molinari. But leaders of the people killed in this clash, as well as whole groups slaughtered, can be counted in hundreds.

So preceding the extreme cases of Sr Dorothy and so many others murdered, there is a permanent struggle permeating the population: on one hand, in areas where the State has not yet managed to establish a presence, where there are no taxes or documents, no police security and a high level of institutional corruption, people are threatened and forced out of their homes. Violent farmers grab land with no justification, arrange their own rights, and extend their properties by force, with the result that the same piece of land can have three or more titles of ownership. On the other hand, these same landowners entice workers from various regions of Brazil, mainly from the interior of the poor, dry north east. So there is an increase in *slave labour*, that scourge hidden within the huge estates. It is in this complicated and violent scenario that Sr Dorothy's death, but before that her missionary life and brilliant initiative, are to be understood.

She came from the north east, from the State of Maranhão, where she had worked with her Sisters of the Congregation of Notre Dame de Namur among the poor country people. Before that, descended from an Irish family, she had moved from the United States to Brazil, inspired by a spirit of mission, leaving behind possibilities of safer work in colleges and institutions to immerse herself in the world of the rural poor. She was something like Mother Teresa of Calcutta to the Brazilian people. But she also had another side to her: she worked to enable the people, women in particular, to become the subjects of their own destiny – which is difficult and, above all, dangerous. Four decades ago, she became a naturalized Brazilian in order to be more radically dedicated to the people. Seeing, however, that the people of her north-eastern area of Maranhão were migrating to the Amazonian region of Pará, she agreed with the Sisters of the Congregation that they had to uproot themselves and go with the migrants. So, after travelling through different parts of Pará, experiencing suffering and persecutions along with the people, they settled in Anapu, in the 'middle ground', on public land – so belonging to the State – some four hundred miles from Belém. They came to a land of forest and conflicts, at the invitation of the bishop of the diocese of Altamira, Erwin Krautler. He is one of the three Catholic bishops who feature among the more than two hundred people explicitly under threat of death in the State of Pará. With the bishop's support and in collaboration with INCRA (the National Institute for Settlement and Agrarian Reform), Sr Dorothy succeeded in having the public lands of the region made over to the PDS, her project for sustainable development. The project aims basically to cultivate 20 per cent of the land and to preserve 80 per cent as forest, using 'forest management' and respecting its incalculable biodiversity, with extractive cultivation and increasing the native species of trees that produce fruits and other harvests. Implementation of such projects gained the support of civic bodies, of organs of state and national government, including the Ministry of the Environment, of universities, and of social movements and pastoral plans. And they began to produce fruit and hope.

But then the confrontations began: *'grileiros'* (farmers who take possession of land using violence, falsifying documents and forcing the inhabitants off) advanced into the same areas. They met with organized and articulate resistance from the people, with juridical battles in the state capital. And they decided to eliminate Sr Dorothy. It later became clear that those who organized her assassination formed a 'consortium': they got together to pay a considerable sum to a middleman who, in his turn, contracted the young gunmen and sold Sr Dorothy's life for fifty reals (some twenty US dollars).

At her funeral celebration, in Anapu, one of the Sisters from her Congregation said, in front of the Environment Minister of Brazil, two bishops, and the people, 'We are not going to bury, we are going to *plant* Sr Dorothy'. In fact her name means 'gift of God', and she is a gift to the Amazonian forest and peoples. Her seed has not ceased producing fruits: her struggle for integration between forest and people has spread through the whole of Brazil. In the State of Pará the 'Dorothy Committee' has been formed, to work together with other bodies and persons of good will: lawyers, religious, politicians, academics, and many young people. The Dorothy Committee operates on various fronts: raising awareness, denunciations, projects, and support for actions promoting the forest and the peoples of the forest. In this way, many are carrying on Sr Dorothy's *dream*. There are in truth many virtually anonymous 'Dorothys' in the region. One of the greatest successes has been the extension of elements of the PDS into the whole of native Brazil, through the actions of the Environment Minister: 80 per cent of the forests must now, by law, be preserved, with forest management, throughout the whole country. This is a great fruit, as big as Brazil, and it come from little, gentle Sr Dorothy, firm and loving to the end, even to her assassins.

The assassins were arrested, but they were not the only ones: the middleman and the chief proponent of the assassination were also brought to court. The Dorothy Committee followed the case closely, to ensure that the law meted out exemplary punishment in order to lessen the impunity with which violence is done to the people and forest in the region. Although all were condemned at their first trial, their resources and changes to accounts of the assassination led to scandalous absolutions, which have, at least for the time being, made the application of real justice impossible – as happens in most cases of assassination in the region. Now the documentary film 'Why they killed Sister Dorothy', directed by a young American, has also exposed this aspect of the mockery made of justice. It even documents the attempt made by the counsel for the man who ordered the crime to make people believe that she was an American infiltrated by the CIA. And the comment by the trial judge: 'Sister Dorothy is not an American or a Brazilian citizen; she is a world citizen'.

In fact, my concluding reflection, theological in nature, has to do with this statement: Sr Dorothy can be recognized as a new paradigm of holiness and martyrdom at a time when Mother Earth is becoming part of spirituality and justice. What defines Christian holiness is love, and what defines Christian martyrdom is love given to the end, *usque ad sanguinem*. In witness to faith in Christ, *propter Christum*, is traditionally added. Nevertheless, *Concilium* has on two occasions (163, *Martyrdom Today*, 1983; 2003/1, *Rethinking Martyrdom*) dealt with the 'jesuanic' martyrdom of those who, following Christ, inspired by his word and his Spirit, gave their lives and their blood *propter Regnum* – for the same cause, that is, as Christ shed his blood for. An example would be Archbishop Oscar Romero, assassinated not explicitly 'out of hatred of the Christian faith' but 'out of hatred of the justice' desired by God and Christ. It might seem a sophism to state that God loves justice to his creatures more than faith in himself, that this is proper to God's pure and non-narcissistic love. Indeed, it was in the one and the same act of love of God that Sr Dorothy loved God's creatures as God loves them.

In Sr Dorothy's martyrdom, something is added historically to Jesus himself, something that could not have occurred to Jesus in his time and place: hatred of Mother Earth through her desecration, through violent and unjust appropriation, added to hatred of the sons and daughters of Earth, hatred of the people who live on the land. She, on the other hand, loved the people and the forest, biodiversity and justice, with one and the same love, her love of God. She ended by helping to overthrow, or at least shake, the ranks of profiteers who desecrate the temple of Creation and make the people desolate. And for that she was executed. Her life and death in the following of Jesus bring something new into Jesus himself: Creation, with its biodiversity, its sons and daughters, takes in the Kingdom of God and his justice, and makes the gift of life and death worth while. This is why the people of Amazonia pray: 'Sister Dorothy, with your open smile and gentle voice, pray for us!'

Translated by Paul Burns

An Tairseach: a Dominican Response to Ecological Awareness[1]

MARIAN O'SULLIVAN

An Tairseach is a project of the Irish Dominican Congregation, established in Wicklow, Ireland, in 1997. It is an Ecology Centre within the setting of an organic/biodynamic farm and conservation area for wildlife. Its purpose is to educate young and old about life on this beautiful planet that is in danger of extinction. We believe that we are at present experiencing a major extinction of species comparable to the one that happened 65 million years ago, when the dinosaurs as well as many of the then known species were wiped out. This extinction, if it continues, will cause the ecology of earth to break down unless we, as a species, undergo a change of mind and heart, cease ravaging the earth with our consumerist policies and practices and become a more benign presence on the planet. The name An Tairseach (the threshold) implies a hope that we are on the brink of a new era when humans will realize that, while we are intimately connected to the earth, we cannot control earth's processes. We are participants in her life rather than lords of creation. This newly developed learning centre at An Tairseach is a response to the needs of our times and has grown out of a long tradition of education carried out by the Irish Dominican Sisters.

I. Setting An Tairseach in a Dominican context

The Irish Congregation, popularly known as the Cabra Dominicans, has its roots in seventeenth-century Galway and over time has spread its branches to other parts of Ireland as well as to several countries abroad. The circumstances of its foundation were, however, far from auspicious. Post-Reformation Ireland under English rule was a place of political turmoil. Yet it was in those circumstances that a group of women who frequented the Dominican church in Galway, wishing to live the religious life, sought and received approval as a community of nuns from the Irish Provincial Chapter of Friars held in Kilkenny in 1643. During the terrible years of Cromwellian persecution, the nuns did all they could to support the needy, but by 1652 it was obvious that they had either to renounce their religious vows and live as lay people or go into exile. They chose exile. More than thirty years later, in 1686, when Catholic King James II had come to the throne in England, two of them, Julian Nolan and Mary Lynch, were invited by the Dominican Provincial to return to Galway to refound the community.

The vast majority of the population at that time was Catholic and poor, though some from the business and professional classes would have been better off. Responding to these particular needs around them, the nuns established schools for the poor who lived in the vicinity of the convents as well as boarding schools for those far from home. Later on in Cabra, Dublin, they were alerted to the presence of children who were profoundly deaf and immediately sent two of the nuns to Caen in France to be trained in the methods of teaching deaf children.[2] For the Sisters, their pulpit was the classroom where young minds and hearts were formed to live with integrity, using their freedom progressively as they grew into adulthood.

II. Setting *An Tairseach* in a twenty-first-century context

At the beginning of the twenty-first century, the challenges that confront us are as many and urgent as those that confronted our founding mothers in penal times in Galway. While some people live in luxury, others are suffering untold hardship as a result of poverty, war, disease, and natural disasters. Our systems are not working. Institutions, whether political, social, or religious, are unable or unwilling to address the problems in any comprehensive way. Ever since the astronauts, on a journey to the moon, saw Earth as a whole for the first time, there has been a growing awareness that our planet is very small, very beautiful, and very fragile. The notion that it can rightly be carved up into sovereign states that have absolute rights to extract its minerals, create hazardous waste, burn its fossil fuels, pollute its air and water, and change its climate is no longer tenable. Climate change is now widely recognized as a serious threat to the future of the planet. A radical re-thinking of the role of the human in the cosmic scheme of things is urgently needed, and a radical restructuring is required. Ecologist Thomas Berry says:

> The Earth simply cannot sustain the burden imposed upon it. The air in many places has become polluted. The water of the planet is toxic for an indefinite period of time. The soils of the Earth are saturated with

chemicals. We have only the slightest idea of the consequences for the physical and psychic life of the human community, especially for the children who have lived in this chemically saturated environment since the day of their conception.

Physical degradation of the natural world is also the degradation of the interior world of the human. To cut the old-growth forests is not simply to destroy the last 5 per cent of the primordial forests left in this country. It is to lose the wonder and majesty, the poetry, music, and spiritual exaltation evoked by such awesome experience of the deep mysteries of existence. It is a loss of soul even more than a loss of lumber or a loss of money."[3]

The question this raised was: Do we Dominicans, as an Order committed to study and the search for truth, have any role in this urgent need for action? The study of our origins would suggest that we do, for there is much in the values of our Dominican tradition that is relevant to our current challenges. Both Albert the Great and Thomas Aquinas, for example, who developed new theological perspectives and approaches in their time, provide important insights, and model for us a courageous openness to new thinking.

As Dominicans committed to the search for truth, we have come to believe that we should be raising our awareness about our intimate connection to the earth, about our responsibility to care for this planet, that we should be challenging destructive practices, both our own and those of others including the large corporations. Further challenged by Pope John Paul II's exhortation that, 'Christians in particular [should] realize that their responsibility within creationand their duty towards nature and the Creator are an essential part of their faith,[4] we realized that this was indeed a religious issue, and that we should also be promoting awareness among other church people. The Sisters therefore decided to take action.

At their 1992 General Chapter the Sisters committed themselves, individually and as a community, to 'support and advance the call to protect the earth' by deepening their own understanding and, by using their skills as educators as well as their resources, to promote this awareness in the wider community.[5] Out of this decision *An Tairseach* was born. The convent in Wicklow, with its 70-acre farm, offered the ideal location. Since 1870 the Wicklow convent had offered education at primary and secondary level and still has about 1,000 students on the campus. Careful planning took place over some years: this involved the collaborative action of Dominican Sisters and some local people, as well as exchange visits to and from Genesis Farm, an ecological learning centre founded in New Jersey by the Caldwell Dominican

Sisters in the United States. The Wicklow project began to take shape: it would be three-pronged, encompassing an organic/biodynamic farm, a conservation area for wildlife, and a study centre for ecology and spirituality.

The first phase involved clearing the land of chemicals – a two-year effort – and conversion to an organic farm system. Once the farm was certified as organic, vegetables were grown and sold through the farm shop. At the same time, development of the conservation area began. This involved the planting of 8,000 trees, the preservation of wetlands, the clearing of a stream, improvement of hedgerows, and the laying of walkways. A pond was established, wild flowers were planted in meadows, and surveys taken of birds, moths, dragonflies, and wild flowers. Many local people helped with this work and gradually a community developed around *An Tairseach*.

To promote thoughtful and life-giving immersion in these surroundings, a programme of activities and rituals was developed to assist people in both mind and heart to be more in tune with the natural rhythm of the seasons. Though we may think that in our modern life we can have warmth and light at the flick of a switch, it is important to realize that we are using up the non-renewable resources of the planet at an alarming rate and that we are utterly dependent on the solar system and particularly our planet Earth for our life, our sustenance, and our health.

The third part of the project was development of the centre for ecology and spirituality. Located in refurbished buildings on the campus, the centre provides classroom and conference space as well as overnight accommodation. Here we offer a full programme of courses for adults and children, which could broadly be described as covering ecology and spirituality. In our offerings, we seek to make available to people the best current scientific knowledge of how our wondeful universe came to be, and our place in it. We share the insights of twentieth-century prophets such as Teilhard de Chardin in the West and Sri Aurobindo in the East, who saw that the unfolding of the universe is both a physical and spiritual evolution. They and others show us convincingly that spirit and matter are two sides of the one coin. They are inseparable. So we are brought full circle, to confront, as Dominic did, the falsity of dualism – the very heresy the Order was founded to combat – , to reclaim the ancient truth that all is one, and that all of creation is good. If Dominic were alive today, he would without doubt be calling on his followers, both women and men, to become fully cognisant of the insights of modern science and to reflect on them in their search for truth.

At *An Tairseach*, therefore, we try to offer people a holistic experience. Within the context of a working organic farm, people see how vegetables are grown without the use of artificial chemicals, cattle are raised out of doors except in extreme weather, enjoying the lush grass of the farm and suckling their own young, The food served in the dining room comes from the farm as far as possible and is prepared with care and eaten with gratitude. Wildlife habitats are preserved and enhanced so as to witness to the importance of making every effort to counteract the loss of bio-diversity being caused by modern farming methods as well as creeping housing development. The courses offered can vary from *Growing Organic Vegetables*, *Vegetarian Cooking*, *Developing a School Garden*, and *Renewable Energy Solutions* to *Spirituality through Art*, *Sacred Dance*, or *Meditation*, or they may just offer people an opportunity to reflect on the interconnectedness of all creation in a beautiful setting of sea, mountains, streams, and woodlands.

Other courses are more explicitly philosophical and intellectual in approach. These provide an opportunity to explore theology and spirituality in the context of our evolving universe, the danger to our planet, and the challenge of living more sustainably on the earth while adapting to an oil-poor future.

To involve the whole body and to engage the deeper aesthetic senses, we use ritual, art, music, and movement to help us internalize our questions and our experience. For example, there is the 'cosmic garden', which marks the major moments in the epic of evolution on a spiral on the ground. We invite people to 'walk' this spiral path, to gain some sense of the vastness of the time it took the earth to create first the stars, then the planets including planet Earth, and finally, to burst forth into life itself.

Embracing and suffusing all of these aspects of our programme at *An Tairseach* is the wisdom of the mystics. We reflect upon the insights of Pierre Teilhard de Chardin, Hildegard of Bingen, and Julian of Norwich; and within our own Dominican tradition, we seek to reclaim the wisdom of Meister Eckhart, who, echoing Thomas Aquinas, insisted that 'All creatures are the utterance of God'.[6] Nor are these mystical insights foreign to the traditions of our Celtic forebears; they too came to a knowledge of the divine through their intimacy with nature long before God became incarnate in Jesus. In fact, because of this awareness of God's presence in the whole of creation, Irish churches in the early Christian period were very small since worship normally took place out of doors in the presence of nature in spite of inclement weather. Those were less pampered times. Reminding us of our heritage from those times is the nearby monastery of Glendalough: we are blessed to live less than half an hour's drive from this historic centre, one of Ireland's most sacred monastic sites, dating from the sixth century.

These are the features, then, that shape our programmes at *An Tairseach*.[7] Through them we seek to discharge our Dominican responsibity to highlight the search for truth as essential for all humans if we are to live up to our calling as the self-conscious dimension of planet Earth. No other species has that responsibility. For us, therefore, not to include the insights of modern scientific discovery in our quest would be a betrayal of trust. We are both encouraged and challenged in our continuing quest by the words of Elizabeth Johnson:

> The neglect of 'the cosmos' by recent decades of mainstream Catholic theology has two deleterious results. It enfeebles theology in its basic task of interpreting the whole of reality in the light of faith, thereby compromising the intellectual integrity of theology. And it blocks what should be theology's powerful contribution to the religious praxis of justice and mercy for a threatened earth, so necessary at this moment of our planet's unprecedented ecological crisis, thereby endangering the moral integrity of theology.[8]

In doing our small part to redress this neglect of the cosmos at *An Tairseach*, we recognize that we are collaborating with growing numbers of committed persons around the globe who are also moving us into the ecological age.

Notes

1. This essay appeared first in *Towards the Intelligent Use of Liberty: Dominican Approaches in Education*, edited by Gabrielle Kelly, OP, and Kevin Saunders, OP, Adelaide: ATF Press, 2007, reprinted here with permission. For the purpose of publication in *Concilium*, I have made several revisions.
2. The School for Deaf Children which they founded in Cabra in 1846 was the 'first Catholic Institution in the U.K. for the deaf': *Annals of Dominican Convent Cabra 1647–1912*, p.108.
3. Thomas Berry, *The Great Work*, New York: Bell Tower, 1999, p. 110.
4. Message of His Holiness Pope John Paul II: World Day of Peace, 1 January 1990, 13.
5. *Acts of the Thirteenth General Chapter of the Congregation of Dominican Sisters*, Cabra, 7
6. Meister Eckhart, *Selected Writings*, trans. Oliver Davies, London: Penguin, 1994, Sermon DW 2, 53
7. For up-to-date information cf www.ecocentrewicklow.ie
8. Elizabeth Johnson, CSJ, 'Presidential Address to the Catholic Theological Society of America, 1995'.

Ethical Management of Natural Resources

I. One home Earth

The constituents of the universe are galaxies, solar systems, stars, and planets. Many galaxies constitute a universe. In our universe, there are about120 billion galaxies. Each galaxy has 200 to 400 billion stars. But how many universes are there? The string theory 'portrays the constituents of nature as tiny wriggling strings, an elegant idea that in principle explains all the forces of nature but in practice leads to *at least 10^{500} potential universes*'.[1] Our universe is just one tiny bubble in a large froth of universes. In the Milky Way our solar system is tucked in a peripheral location and does not occupy a central position. In the centre of the galaxy there is a massive black hole which does not permit even light to pass through.

It has been agreed by cosmologists that the age of the cosmos may be around 13.7 billion light years. The number of extra-solar planets increases with every human quest to locate another suitable earth like ours. Of the 347 extra-solar planets, Earth is the only planet suitable for human life.[2] In our solar system, Earth is the only planet situated in the 'Habitable Zone'. The ecological conditions present on Earth are ideally suited to sustain life and therefore there is only *one earth* in this 'multiverse' where plant life, animal life, and human life are possible. Although the universe is vast and dynamic, life and intelligent life are found only on Planet Earth (as far as science can tell us now). Hence, Earth is the only 'Biosphere' that can sustain life

II. Water and food

Biosphere is filled with natural substances. A natural substance becomes a natural resource when humans find a useful application. Three natural resources attain the status of vital (life) resources. They are: (i) land, (ii) water, and (iii) air.[3] Natural resources can be divided into three categories:

(1) Natural eco-systems with natural resources that can be divided into two broad sections: (i) renewable resources such as plants; (ii) non-renewable resources such as fossil fuels (natural gas, coal, and oil);

(2) Man-made resources such as currency, education, electricity, medicine, cement, concrete and other public utilities such as sanitation and portable water.

(3) Human Resources – humans with bio-ethical perspective with regard to natural resources.[4]

The importance of water

Water is a nation's lifeline, precious natural wealth, and it is the common resource for all humanity. The 1948 Universal Declaration on Human Rights (Article 25) recognizes the right to life as the basis of human rights. Hence, it is understood universally that without 'the right to water' there is no 'right to life'. Gorbacheve (2007) recognized, 'Water is the most important single element needed in order for people to achieve the universal human right to "a standard of living adequate for the health and well-being of himself and his family" (Article 25, Universal Declaration of Human Rights). Without access to clean water, health and well-being are not only severely jeopardized, they are impossible: people without basic water supplies live greatly reduced and impoverished lives – with little opportunity to create better futures for their children'. *The Stockholm Declaration of the United Nations on Human Environment* endorses this: 'The natural resources of the earth, including the air, water, land, flora and fauna and especially representative samples of natural systems, must be safeguarded for the benefit of present and future generations through careful planning or management, as appropriate. . . . Nature conservation including wildlife must therefore receive importance in planning for economic development'. Finally, legal systems also underline such a basic concept: 'Rivers, forests, minerals and such other resources constitute a nation's natural wealth. These resources are not to be frittered away and exhausted by any one generation. Every generation owes a duty to all succeeding generations to develop and conserve the natural resources of the nation in the best possible way. It is in the interest of mankind. It is in the interest of the nation.'[5]

Water is not a renewable resource. *But it is a recyclable resource* through its global cycle. Moreover, the amount of water (1,400 million Km³) in the biosphere is fixed (finite). If 'x' amount of water was present in the 1950s to quench the thirst of 1 billion people then the same amount (x) has to be shared by 6 billion people in 2009. Logically, *per capita* consumption of water will fall proportionately by 2030 when the population reaches 8 billion people. Rarity of a natural resource incites violence. Water is a one-time allotted resource. When resources dwindle distributive justice will be offset. People have now started to speak about 'water war'! Water is found in four pockets: (i) five oceans and seas (about 97.44%); (ii) polar ice caps (about 2%); (iii) fresh water in rivers and lakes (0.6% – less than 1%); and (iv) as groundwater (8 million Km³ = 0.2%). In rivers and lakes only 0.25 geograms of water are found (0.0004%). If water in sections (i) to (iii) can be contained in a one-gallon jar then the remaining fresh water is only one spoonful.[6] Fresh water, as a very rare natural resource, needs judicial–bio-ethical–spiritual management.

Food crops: narrow choice-set

Of a total of about 3,000,000 plants only about 120–140 plants are edible. But the actual choice becomes narrower: only about 20 food crops can provide 80% energy, while only 10 crops are commonly used by humans. Finally, there are only three staple food crops (rice, wheat, and corn) for human sustenance.[7] The global food scenario for humans is placed in a food-crop-resource-limited setting.

India, since its independence in 1947, has done remarkably well in food grain production. During 1947, India produced about 50 million metric tons of food grain to feed its 300 million people, when the world population was about 1 billion. India is now producing about 230.67 (2007–8) million metric tones of grain to feed its 1.2 billion people, which is 13.39 million tones of food more than the amount produced (217.28) during 2006–2007.[8] Such an enhanced food production is at the cost of soil degradation – healthy land has become saline.[9] At this critical point food grain production is levelling off: *i.e.*, increased supply is just sufficient to meet the demand. Then there is a mismatch between population growth rate (1.9%) and the percentage of increased production (1.2%). Also, the 'World Food Program' report estimates that India harbours more than a fourth of the world's hungry mouths, *i.e.*, about 230 million people. Moreover, States within India, such as Madhya Pradesh, may pose an extremely difficult food insecurity situation since its Global Hunger Index is similar to that of Chad or Ethiopia.[10] Such warnings about food insecurity have been given year after year.

By 2025, the grain production rate has to be doubled. A second green revolution is necessary. 'We need to achieve new breakthroughs, and scale new heights'.[11] The warning about food insecurity has been given year after year. In 2007 UNFAO sent an additional alarm signal: 'In an "unforeseen and unprecedented" shift, the world food supply is dwindling rapidly and food prices are soaring to historic levels. . . .' Such a situation may create 'a very serious risk that fewer people will be able to get food'.[12] It has been predicted that when the Indian population touches 1.5 billion in 2030/50 there will be a further deficiency of about (minus) 45 million metric tones of food grains.[13] There are many risk factors in stretching the land beyond its production capacity! A risk is a hazard which is about to happen – but waiting is the biggest risk.

Collateral Risks

In order to enhance food grain production a wide range of insecticides, herbicides, and fungicides is used; these are known to cause endocrine disruption due to the presence of dioxins, PCBs, and DDT. The freshwater mussel, *Elliptio complanata*, is affected by the weed-killer *Atrazine* and the insecticide *Bifenthrin*, which initiates the production of yolk protein *vitellogenin*, just like the female hormone oestrogen.[14] In environmental toxicology, these chemicals are designated as 'environmental mimics' of the hormone oestrogen. As a result there is a sexual transformation, which causes populations to undergo shifts in sexual composition toward an increased number of females. This is the process of feminization of males. In the male catfish, *Clarias ganepinus*, of South African reservoirs, primary oocytes were found to be scattered in testicular tissue, initiating a sexual transformation through inter-sexuality of inter-sex regime.[15]

Genetically Modified Crops

Introduction of genetically modified (GM) food crops to combat food insecurity is yet another answer. But there are many risks in GM crops. The possibility also exists that too much genetic manipulation of rice may finally eliminate rice from our food-list. The risk of hunger and malnutrition will become much more severe than we expect.

In order to enhance grain production many bio-technology companies are engaged in developing herbicide-resistant food crops, which are genetically modified. These transgenic crops will only increase the use of herbicides and insecticides. These chemicals will be found in the food chain and in water run-off. Monsanto has developed 'Roundup-Ready' transgenic (GM-food) crops, such as soya beans and legumes, that are resistant to pesticides. Other plants that are not Roundup Ready will succumb to the pesticide, a feature that only increases the use of pesticides. In GM crops the gene activity for tryptophan amino acid is increased, which triggers the production of by-products such as isoflavonoids. These isoflavonoids exhibit a remarkable functional similarity to human oestrogens, and hence they are called the phytoestrogens.[16] These phytoestrogens – 'Ecoestrogens and Xenoestrogens' (Xeno = alien) – can produce decreases in sperm count, precocious puberty, and breast cancer. High oestrogenic activity in males will result in lower sperm count, and in females it advances the age at which puberty occurs.

III. Toward a unisex society?

The growing number of oestrogen mimics in the environment has been linked to early puberty in girls. The normal, average age of onset is between twelve and thirteen. A recent study of 17,000 girls in the United States indicated that 7 per cent of white and 27 per cent of black girls exhibited physical signs of puberty by age seven. For ten-year-old girls, the percentages increased to 68 and 95, respectively. Studies from the United Kingdom, Canada, and New Zealand have shown similar changes in the age of puberty onset.[17]

All this has collateral impacts. It produces sterile males. Couples with no prospects of child-bearing will seek medically Assisted Reproductive Technology (ART). In a unisex population with infertile couples there is the option of generating a child technologically which may raise many epigenetic consequences of ART.

IV. Future Prospects

The eco-theological contributions of Rev William Buckland (1784–1856), Pierre Teilhard de Chardin (1881–1955), and Lynn White, Jr (1907–1987) have prepared Christianity to accept the theory of Evolution. In September 2008 the Church of England apologized posthumously to Darwin for its 'anti-evolutionary fervour'. Commenting on the apology letter, the Vatican reiterated its earlier doctrinal stand that 'the theory of evolution was com-patible with the Bible'.[18]

Moral problems that emerge due to the rapid advancement of Hi-techno-sciences are many and complex. It remains to be seen how the Church can provide spiritual guidance in areas of ultra-modern biosciences and medical sciences that exhibit a tendency for making 'immoral advances'.[19]

Notes

1. Dennis Overbye, 'Dark, perhaps forever', *New York Times* 3 June 2008 (Online).
2. Cf. 'The Extrasolar Planets Encyclopaedia': http://exoplanet.eu/, 2009.
3. Cf. E. P. Odum, *Fundamentals of Ecology*, Philadelphia, PA: Saunders College Publishing, 1971, p. 574.
4. Cf. J. Azariah, 'Bioethics for Enhanced Sustainability', in J. Azariah, H. Azariah, and D. R. Macer (eds), *Bioethics in India* (Proceedings of the International Bioethics Workshop in India), Christchurch, NZ: Eubios Ethics Institute, 1998, p. 403.
5. Court case, State of Tamil Nadu *versus* M/S Hind Stone (AIR 1981 SC 711).
6. Cf. J. Azariah, 'Emerging Biblical Insights in Bioethics', *Dharma Deepika* 10 (Jan. 2006), 5–23
7. Cf. J. Azariah, 'New Genetics: Food and Bioethics', in *Bioethics and Environment*, ed. M. Gabriel, K. Joshua, and J. Azariah, Chennai: Madras Christian College, 2001, pp. 121–31.
8. Cf. 'India's food grain output at 230 mn tonnes may moderate prices', *Thaindian News*, lead article, 9 July 2008).
9. 'Call for soil research unit', *The Hindu*, 30 Jan. 1998, p. 5.
10. Cf. S. Sengupta, 'As Indian Growth Soars, Child Hunger Persists', *New York Times* 12 March 2009. At http://www.nytimes.com/2009/03/13/world/asia/13malnutrition.html
11. 'Manmohan wants farm output increased to match demands', *The Hindu*, 24 Sept. 2006, p 8.
12. E. Rosenthal, 'World Food Supply is shrinking, U.N. Agency warns', *New York Times*, 18 Dec. 2007. At http://www.nytimes.com/2007/12/18/business/worldbusiness/18supply.html
13. Cf. L. R. Brown, *Who Will Feed China?*, Washington, D.C., Worldwatch Institute,1995, p. 163.
14. Cf. The Free Library, 16. Dec. 2006, *Science News* – 'Pesticides mimic estrogen in shellfish' (Online). Also reported in *Science News* 2 Nov 2002, p. 275, and *Science News* 4 Feb 2006, p 74 (Online).
15. Cf. I. E. G. Barnhoorn, M. S. Bornman, G. M. Pieterse, and J. H. J. van Vuren, 'Histological evidence of intersex in feral sharptooth catfish (*Clarias gariepinus*) from an estrogen-polluted water source in Gauteng, South Africa', *Environ Toxicol* 19 (2004), 603–8.
16. Cf. M. Lappe and B. Bailey, *Against the Grain: Biotechnology and the Corporate Takeover of your Food*, Monroe, ME: Common Courage Press, 1998, p. 164.
17. Cf. K. Morgan, 'Wrong number: Plastic ingredient spurs chromosomal defects', *Science News* 163 (5 Apr. 2003), 213. At http://www.sciencenews.org/articles/20030405/fob6.asp.; HIN Poisons: Plastic. The Health Information Network Online, 2009. At http://72.14.235.132/search?q=cache:http://www.

nzhealth.net.nz/poisons/plastics.shtml
18. New Scientist staff and Reuters, 'Vatican says it does not owe Darwin an apology', Online 17 Sept. 2008.
19. D. Jones, 'Immoral Advances: Is science out of control?', *New Scientist* 2690 (9 Jan. 2009).

A Reflection on World Youth Day 2008

JILL GOWDIE

I write this reflection as a participant in World Youth Day, not an observer. And I write it from participation as a mentor accompanying twenty-five of our young staff from across our school and centre communities. I also write it as a mother whose thirteen-year-old son accompanied his father and me, and who shared his time between us and a very large Italian contingent with which he somehow connected – and has stayed connected. . . .

 Given the multiple entry points to this particular – and any – experience, I have decided to apply some layers of reflection, often used when reading scripture, to interpret my WYD experience, and I offer this in turn for reflection from your own vantage point in relation to the phenomenon that was World Youth Day 2008.

I. The Literal Reading

What happened on the face of things?

Most simply put, the worldwide Catholic Community was informed and encouraged to prepare for a gathering of young people from across the world to be held in Sydney, Australia, in the July of 2008. In Brisbane, a special directorate was set up three years beforehand to coordinate pilgrims both staying here from overseas and going to Sydney for World Youth Day and to coordinate archdiocesan activities in the lead-up, especially the 'Days in the Diocese'. In Sydney, even more feverish activity began about the same time. In all cities on the east coast of Australia, negotiations with governments at all levels were initiated for funds and logistic support during the weeks around World Youth Day and its lead-up and post-WYD events.

In this Archdiocese (Brisbane), all Vicariates mobilized to give focussed support to this event, with implications for sparse funds further stretched across different diocesan offices. A renewal of focus on ministry with young people directed effort into long-term strategies rather than the WYD event itself, aiming to plant opportunities for the future. Parishes and schools invited students and youth groups into an understanding of pilgrimage and the practical preparations for the Sydney gathering. The outlay of monies required to organize activities and pilgrimage groups around such a huge event, along with the massive logistical challenges, weighed heavily on all those involved. In addition, there were fears that we would constitute a major terrorist target, and security measures were heightened because of this.

Nevertheless, energies were gathered and the preparation and formation beforehand were done very well. The Days in the Diocese happened and happened marvellously in Brisbane! The pilgrimage to Sydney and the WYD event there went without incident and was received by the city in general very positively and by the pilgrims enthusiastically. They poured into Sydney, flew the flags, walked the length and breadth of it, filled the trains and buses and ferries with enormous patience and good will. The police and army were overcome by the peacefulness, which translated into no incidents whatsoever on the trains and buses for the week of WYD – unheard of in Sydney.

The structure of catechesis, the Eucharistic celebrations, and the prayer gatherings were clear and well attended. Some of those most vocal in the Australian ecclesial hierarchy claimed a new era of vocational growth. The Pope himself appeared moved by the experience as the days progressed. Photographs and images of bishops, priests, and happy young people filled the papers and televised coverage. In every way, WYD 2008 was deemed a great success.

II. The Christological Reading

What did we understand about Jesus here that showed us how to be more fully human?

Within this sequence of events, the face of Jesus showed itself. One of these faces, the one most photographed, was in the ecclesial body – the Pope, the bishops, the priests, the brothers and nuns; all directly dress-coded if you like to translate the presence of Jesus. However, Jesus was present at least just as powerfully in the faces of the young, who were so open and accepting of all those they met and in the companions who ministered to them – the larger group of the body of Christ. I saw it in the circle of young people, all strangers to each other, spontaneously falling into song with each other. I saw it in small groups sitting wherever they found a piece of ground – Australians listening to the unbelievable, painful reality of life being shared by a pilgrim they may have just met, eyes fixed compassionately on each other. I saw it in one of our Australian bishops sharing the story of his journey with the indigenous of our land. I saw it in an Australian girl in old jeans with a European priest in clerical black dancing with joy down the street. I saw it in two young men squatting down, sharing their food, and listening to three homeless men during the night. I saw it in the shining face of my son who had connected up with a tribe of Italians he'd met in Brisbane in the Days in the Diocese, and realized his heart beat with a fire like theirs. I saw it in the tiny barefoot aboriginal woman, swamped on stage by official dignitaries, who held thousands mesmerized with her Holy Spirit story.

The gospel vision of Jesus and the fruits of the Spirit were so tangible, you could almost touch them. Love, forgiveness, compassion, joy, peace . . . these shone genuinely in the being of the pilgrims and spilled into the general public. The transformation of the Sydneysiders – and the Pope – was palpable. Sydneysiders changed from wary, if not hostile 'tolerators' of the imposition of WYD on their daily life to smiling, even eager conversational supporters as they were swept up by the sheer joy and openness of this ocean of young people. The Pope himself appeared to transform from a slightly wary, reserved visage to a far more open smiling presence by the final days of the week. He too was swept up by the power of these young people. This sense of human connection, of real communion, is fruit of the Spirit of Jesus – humanity so in tune with God that relationships are changed all around us.

III. The Mystical Reading

What do we understand about the heart of God and the movement of the Spirit from this?

We understand anew what is at the heart of communion – that we learn who we are through the eyes of each other; that we follow best in Jesus' footsteps when we meet each other where we are, not where we are expected to be; that to hear each other's stories into life is a most powerful, respectful, and transformative act of human solidarity, and a sure path to the heart of God. Again I am reminded of Karl Rahner's clarion call to the future Church to be mystics or risk being nothing at all. My work and my experience constantly resonate with the truth of this, and WYD08 confirmed its reality.

We understand anew that the Spirit will blow where she will – the deepest success of WYD could not be measured in clerical inches; it was a deep flowing energy of the heart that will not be tethered. Neither is this the superficial rapture of too many young people given too much hype. It was an extraordinary sense of oneness that lived beneath the timetable of events, and it was best seen and felt in a thousand unfilmed moments. It is a reality that lives and blossoms almost in spite of the attempts to cordon and shape and drive it, that thrives underneath and beyond respectfully holding the particular ecclesial idiosyncrasies of the age.

And we recognize all this as the mystical reality of God's love. A communion that is true, honest, and consuming of other things in its path. This was the untold story of WYD for me. And it meant that despite encountering some very disturbing moments with a few overseas clerics, my sense of hope and joy in the future of the Church was stronger than ever.

IV. Transforming Action

What change is invoked as we engage with the world?

I am left with a sense of trust in the Spirit. As Sara laughed in surprise at the possibilities of what God can do, so do I. I am left with a sense of pride and utter belief that the Church's ministry in Catholic education is in good hands in our young staff. Their individual faith journeys through the week were a privilege to companion. They will live the Good News with integrity and energy. And they already are!

And I am left with a sense that young people really are the hope of the world.

These realizations change the heavy sense of responsibility so many of us carry about the future, and the life of the Church. It is good to be reminded that it is never really just up to us. As our Celtic forebears knew, God is present, bidden or unbidden.

Contributors

ELAINE WAINWRIGHT is Professor of Theology and Head of the School of Theology at the University of Auckland, New Zealand. She is a New Testament scholar with a particular interest in a range of contextual hermeneutics including feminist, ecological, and post-colonial. Her most recent research was in gender and healing in the Greco-Roman world and early Christianity, and she is turning now to developing an ecological hermeneutic for reading the Gospel of Matthew.

Address: School of Theology, University of Auckland, 24 Princes Street, Auckland, New Zealand
E-mail: em.wainwright@auckland.ac.nz

LEONARDO BOFF was born in 1938 and is currently Emeritus Professor of Theology and Ethics at the State University of Rio de Janeiro. He is a member of the *Letter from the Earth* initiative and joint editor of its journal. He was awarded the Alternative Nobel Peace Prize by the Swedish Parliament in 2001 and is the author of more than 70 books in the fields of theology, ethics, spirituality and ecology, many of which have been translated into English.

Address: Caixa Postal 92144, Itaipava–25741-970, Petrópolis–RJ– Brazil
E-mail: lboff@leonardoboff.com

ANNE ELVEY is a researcher and poet. Her current work in eco-criticism and biblical studies is supported by the Centre for Comparative Literature and Cultural Studies, Monash University. Author of *An Ecological Feminist Reading of the Gospel of Luke: A Gestational Paradigm* (2005), she is working on a book to be titled *The Matter of the Text*. She is convenor of a cross-institutional inter-disciplinary eco-theology and eco-spirituality research group, based at Melbourne College of Divinity.

Address: 5 Maranoa Crescent, Coburg VIC 3058, Australia.
E-mail: aelvey@tpg.com.au

FELIX WILFRED was born in Tamil Nadu, India in 1948. He is the President of the Faculty of Arts and Chairman of the School of Philosophy and Religious Thought at the State University of Madras. He is also a member of the Statutory Ethical Committee of the Indian Institute of Technology, Madras. He was a member of the International Theological Commission of the Vatican. As visiting professor, he has taught at the universities of Nijmegen, Münster, Frankfurt, Boston College, and Ateneo de Manila. His researches and field studies today cut across many disciplines in humanities and social sciences. His more recent publications in the field of theology are *On the Banks of Ganges* (²2002), *Asian Dreams and Christian Hope* (²2003), *The Sling of Utopia: Struggles for a Different Society* (2005), and *Margins: Site of Asian Theologies* (2008).

Address: University of Madras, Dept. of Christian Studies, Chepauk, Madras 600 005, India
E-mail: felixwilfred@gmail.com

ALIRIO CÁCERES AGUIRRE is a permanent deacon in the Archdiocese of Bogotá in Colombia. He has an engineering degree in Eco-enviromentalism as well as specializing in education and holding a Master's in Theology. He lectures and researches at the Faculty of Theology at the Javeriana Pontifical University, where he directs the 'Eco-theology' research team as well as acting as consultant to environmental, pedagogical, and pastoral projects. His Master's thesis on epistemological presuppositions and methodological criteria for a relevant ecological pastoral strategy is in course of publication.

Address: Pontificia Universidad Javeriana, Facultad de Teología, Carrera 5 numero 39-00 Edificio Arrupe – piso 2, Bogotá, Colombia
E-mail: acaceres@javeriana.edu.co

JACQUES HAERS was born in 1956 and is a Jesuit, currently teaching systematic theology at the K. U. Leuven Faculty of Theology, where he chairs the Centre for Liberation Theologies. He is also a member of OCIPE, Brussels, and its Ignatian Ecological Network.

Address: Windmolenveldstraat 44, B-3000 Leuven, Belgium
E-mail: jacques.haers@theo.kuleuven.be or jacques@jesuits.net

NEIL DARRAGH is currently engaged in theological research and community development. He is an adjunct lecturer and research supervisor in the School of Theology, University of Auckland, and in the Catholic Institute of Theology, New Zealand.

Address: 16 Waterloo Quadrant, Auckland City 1010, New Zealand.
E-mail: n.darragh@auckland.ac.nz

MARY JUDITH RESS, a U.S. Catholic lay missionary with Maryknoll, has been living and working in Latin America (El Salvador, Peru, and Chile) since 1970. She holds a doctorate in Feminist Theology from the San Francisco Theological School in California, and Master's degrees in Political Economics from the Graduate School of Social Research in New York and in Spanish Language and Literature from the Universidad Internacional in Saltillo, Mexico. Her writings include *Ecofeminism in Latin America* (2006, which won second place in best gender issues at the Catholic Press Association of the US and Canada in 2007), *Lluvia para florecer: Entrevistas sobre el ecofeminismo en América Latina* (2002), *Circling in, Circling out: A Con-spirando Reader* (2005), *Vírgenes y diosas en América Latina: La resignificación de lo sagrado* (with Veronica Cordero, Graciela Pujol, and Coca Trillini, 2004), *Del Cielo a la Tierra: una antología de teología feminista* (with Ute Seibert and Lene Sjorup, 1994).

Address: Casa Central de Maryknoll, Casilla 204, Correo 17, Santiago, Chile.
E-mail: judyress@yahoo.com

JOHN CLAMMER is Professor of Development Sociology and Director of International Courses at the United Nations University, Tokyo. He was previously Professor of Comparative Sociology and Asian Studies at Sophia University, Tokyo, from 1989 to 2007. Prior to that he taught at the University

of Hull and the National University of Singapore and was a visiting professor at a number of universities in the UK, Australia, Germany, Japan, Korea,
and Argentina. He works in the fields of development sociology, the sociology of culture and the sociology of religion. The author of a number of books
and many papers, his most recent major work is the book *Diaspora and Belief:
Globalization, Religion and Identity in Postcolonial Asia* (2009).

Address: John Clammer, Office of the Rector, United Nations University,
53-70 Jingumae 5-chome, Shibuya-ku, Tokyo 150-8925, Japan.
E-mail: clammer@hq.unu.edu

JOSIAS DA COSTA JÚNIOR was born in Rio de Janeiro, and holds a degree in
Literature. He teaches Religious Sciences and is a Doctor in Theology at
the Pontifcal Catholic University of Rio de Janeiro. He is also Professor of
Theology and History at the Bennett Methodist University Centre (RJ)
and is co-author of *Religião em diálogo. Considerações interdisciplinares sobre
religião, cultura e sociedade* (2008).

Address: Rua Marques de Abrantes, 55 – Flamengo – Rio de Janeiro, RJ
– Brasil
E-mail: josiasdacosta@gmail.com.

LUIZ CARLOS SUSIN is Professor of Systematic Theology at the Pontifical
Catholic University of Rio Grande do Sul and at the Higher School of
Theology and Franciscan Spirituality, both in Porto Alegre, Brazil. He is an
ex-president of the Brazilian Society for Theology and Religious Studies,
and secretary general of the World Forum for Theology and Liberation. His
recent research has been into the relationship between theology and ecology.
His publications include *A Criação de Deus* (2003); *Deus, Pai, Filho e Espirito
Santo; Jesus, Filho de Deus e Filho de Maria; Assim na terre como no céu*, some
published by Paulinas (São Paulo) and some by Vozes (Petrópolis).

Address: Rua Juarez Távora, 171, 91520-100 – Porto Alegre (RS), Brazil
E-mail: lcsusin@pucrs.br

MARIAN O'SULLIVAN is an Irish Dominican Sister. An educator and school
principal for many years in South Africa, she participated in the negotiations
during the apartheid regime to open Catholic schools to all races. As elect-
ed prioress of her Congregation (1986–98), her involvement in education

spanned many countries. She is currently Marian Director of *An Tairseach* at Wicklow, Ireland.

Address: Marian O'Sullivan, Dominican Farm and Ecology Centre, Wicklow Town, Ireland.
E-mail: marian@ecocentrewicklow.ie

DR JAYAPAUL AZARIAH was educated at the Duke Marine Laboratory, North Carolina, USA, holds a Ph.D. degree in Marine Science, and has contributed extensively in the area of Coastal Zone Management. He is the first Indian to receive, since 1920, the prestigious international award from the Plymouth Marine Laboratory, UK, for the year 1991. He served the University of Madras for 38 years and retired as Professor, Head, and Director of its School of Life Sciences. He organized the first International Conference in Bioethics in 1997 and issued the Chennai Statement of Bioethics. He then founded the All India Bioethics Association (AIBA). He is active in promoting international bioethics through serving as President (2007–8; 2008–9) of the Asian Bioethics Association and his editorial involvement in various journals and other publications.

Address: New No.4, 8th Lane, Indiranagar, Chennai 600 020, India
E-mail: jazariah@yahoo.com

JILL GOWDIE is Principal Education Officer, Evangelization and Spiritual Formation, Catholic Education, Archdiocese of Brisbane. She has qualifications across the areas of education, religious education, theology, spirituality, liturgy, and journalism. She brings all of that background to her current doctoral studies in developing a contemporary approach to spiritual formation, currently being completed through Australian Catholic University (ACU). Her teaching experience spans primary, secondary, tertiary, and adult educational contexts. Jill is known in Australia as a facilitator, speaker, and writer in the areas of her professional interests. Since 2006 she has been developing a renewed vision and a new team within Catholic education in the Archdiocese of Brisbane, focusing on evangelization and spiritual formation. Jill is married to Geoff and they have four children.

Address: GPO Box 1201 Brisbane 4001 Qld Australia
E-mail: jgowdie@bne.catholic.edu.au

Concilium Subscription Information

February   2009/1: *Evil Today and Struggles to be Human*

April   2009/2: *Which Religious Heritages for the Future?*

June   2009/3: *Eco-theology*

October   2009/4: *Monotheism? – Divinity and Unity Reconsidered*

December   2009/5: *Fathers of the Church in Latin America*

New subscribers: to receive *Concilium* 2009 (five issues) anywhere in the world, please copy this form, complete it in block capitals and send it with your payment to the address below.

- -

Please enter my subscription for *Concilium* 2009

Individuals	Institutions
____ £40.00 UK	____ £55.00 UK
____ £60.00 overseas	____ £75.00 overseas
____ $110.00 North America/Rest of World	____ $140 North America/Rest of World
____ €99.00 Europe	____ €125.00 Europe

Postage included – airmail for overseas subscribers

Payment Details:
Payment must accompany all orders and can be made by cheque or credit card
I enclose a cheque for £/$/€ _____ Payable to SCM-Canterbury Press Ltd
Please charge my Visa/MasterCard (Delete as appropriate) for £/$/€ _____
Credit card number _____
Expiry date _____
Signature of cardholder _____
Name on card _____
Telephone _____ E-mail _____

Send your order to *Concilium*, SCM-Canterbury Press Ltd
13–17 Long Lane, London EC1A 9PN, UK
E-Mail: office@scm-canterburypress.co.uk

Customer service information:
All orders must be prepaid. Subscriptions are entered on an annual basis (i.e. January to December). No refunds on subscriptions will be made after the first issue of the Journal has been despatched. If you have any queries or require information about other payment methods, please contact our Customer Services department.

www.ingramcontent.com/pod-product-compliance
Lightning Source LLC
Chambersburg PA
CBHW060044030426
42334CB00019B/2485